Mr. Satanism Irreparably Damages Christmas

By Mr. Satanism
(Duh)

©2024 Mr. Satanism. All rights reserved. No portion of this publication may be reproduced or distributed in any manner whatsoever without the express written consent of the publisher, save for brief passages quoted in the context of reviews or scholarly works. Published by Inept Concepts.

Almost published as "Mr. Satanism Comes Up Your Chimney" until marketing talked us out of it. If you're a hot chick though the offer still stands.

This book is dedicated to Eve,
who is so, so, so, *so* fucking fine.

Introduction

If you don't already know what Christmas is, or what movies are, you probably shouldn't be reading this book. If you don't know who Mr. Satanism is, you *definitely* shouldn't be reading this book. Seriously, you're just going to get upset. Consider reading a book about dogs instead. Here's one: *Bob, Son of Battle*, by Alfred Ollivant. It's about this limey douchebag who owns a sheepdog named "Owd Bob" that's so pathologically beloved by everyone that eventually every able-bodied dude in town just lines up and runs a train on the dog, sobbing tears of joy in the process, because *"Lawd o' mercy, 'e's th' Owd Un 'e is!"* At least that's how I assume the book ended. I only got halfway through it, but trust me, it was *clearly* building up to that.

Okay, that was a test. Are you super offended and frothing at the mouth? Did you drive to the jewelry store to buy a strand of pearls just so you can clutch them? If the answer is yes, close this book and walk away right now. Otherwise, turn the page and let's get started...

Ace Venture: Pet Detective "The Reindeer Hunter"
(1995)

Ace Ventura was an annoying piece of shit and I can't believe they made a cartoon out of him, but they did and here's the inevitable Christmas installment. As it opens he's somehow making it snow in his apartment (I guess in this version he has magical powers) when he gets a call from Santa Claus because someone kidnapped his (Santa's) reindeer. If you've ever seen his (Ace Ventura's) movies you know that he generally solves the case by being unbelievably fucking annoying, and that's his approach this time too - he basically just wanders around bothering people until he locates the bad guys by accident. It turns out they kidnapped the reindeer so they could steal their glands by shoving giant needles up their (the reindeers') asses, which I have to admit is pretty unique as far as evil schemes go. The best thing about this video though is when Ace finally confronts them: they just kick the living piss out of him and Santa has to step in to actually save the day. Seeing Ace Ventura on the receiving end of violence is always a winner, but the rest of this cartoon is so lazy it even uses some of the same jokes from the movies; I guess they figured that a fucktard talking with his ass is so goddamn clever that seeing it once just isn't enough. I would say that this cartoon is just as shitty as the movies, but it's only a half hour long so technically that makes it only one third as shitty. That's still almost as bad as finding a mysterious lump in your sack, though, so if you watch this piece of crap don't say I didn't warn you.

Alpha's Magical Christmas
(1994)

This is supposed to be the Mighty Morphin Power Rangers Christmas special, but if you're one of the fucking retards who actually liked that show don't get too excited and piss yourself or anything because the Power Rangers are only in it for like the last two seconds, and even then only about half of them show up. Instead, the focus is on their annoying sidekick. I think he's supposed to be a robot, but he looks like some jackass in a grocery store Halloween costume with an old air filter stuck on his head. He sounds kinda gay, too; why do so many TV shows and movies feature robots that are programmed to be homosexual stereotypes? Think about it: there's this one, C-3PO, Twiki... Twiki even had a "life partner" that looked like a cross between a frying pan and a Lite Brite who he wore around his neck. Remember that? And they used to argue like an old married couple? What the fuck is up with that? Anyway, this particular gay robot is lonely because the Power Rangers can't be on hand for Christmas because the company that produces Power Rangers videos didn't feel like paying them to appear in this one, so he kidnaps a bunch of little kids to hang out with him instead. Then they sing Christmas songs for fifteen minutes. That's the whole show. Am I wrong to expect a Power Rangers special to at least have a bunch of fighting in it? I'll bet tons of kids ended up crying when their parents stuffed their stocking with this piece of fucking shit. Hell, I would've been happy if we just got to see the Pink Ranger in a sexy little Santa outfit, but they can't even manage that. Unbelievable. Kiss my ass, *Alpha's Magical Christmas*.

Amazing Stories "Santa '85"
(1985)

Santa being real and having to deal with real-life shit like burglar alarms and police line-ups had been done so many fucking times (yes, even by 1985) that I can't believe *any* show would trot out such a tired concept again, even one as epically lazy as *Amazing Stories*. Here it is though, but the truly astounding thing is that this is one of the few episodes of this series that's actually okay. It must be because of skill or something. Seriously, whoever made this one knew that it would be the little things that made it work, like when Santa's being arrested but takes the time to smile and wink at the main kid. Christmas could be wholly and permanently fucked, but Santa's immediate concern is that this one kid doesn't get all freaked out, which is exactly the type of thing that Santa Claus would take into consideration. Still, here's the gargantuan, gaping plot hole: Santa makes his rounds every Christmas, right? So why would he suddenly be stymied by a grate blocking a chimney or so ill-prepared to bypass a simple home security system? It's not like this was new shit in 1985. It would be one thing if he just popped into existence or, say, traveled through time, but that's not how they set this up so the only other explanation is that Santa

Claus has the memory of a fucking goldfish. Maybe he needs to do like that cat from *Memento* and tattoo all new, relevant information onto his body as it becomes available. Or, you know, buy a PDA or something.

Useless Trivia: When they re-ran this episode the following year they changed the title to "Santa '85/'86". So are we supposed to take from this that the *exact same thing* happened to Santa two Christmases in a row, and he made the *exact same choices and mistakes* BOTH times? Christ, maybe he should be tested for Alzheimer's or something.

Annie Claus is Coming to Town

(2011)

Why is Santa Claus's daughter always depicted as being so goddamned hot? Not that I'm complaining, mind you, it's just that you'd assume she'd be, well, you know, kinda fat. In this movie she's so fine they had to get the redhead from *Accepted* (2006) to play her, but they do balance this out by making her so obnoxiously chipper that I almost didn't want to fuck her.

So, it seems that it's her time to go out into the real world and see if she likes it better than life at the North Pole (I guess the Clauses are Amish), so she throws a dart at a spinning globe and it lands right on... Los Angeles. Because not enough fucking movies take place there already. For real, could just *one* of you Hollywood assclowns show a little imagination once in a while? I mean, how about having that dart land smack dab in the middle of Algeria? Now *that* would be an interesting movie. Best of all, if you shot it on location maybe some of you wouldn't come back.

As for the plot, well, the pitch was obviously "It's *Elf,* with a hot chick," but it's one thing when it's a 6'3" dude who's hopelessly obsessed with Christmas and naive to the point of retardation, and another thing entirely when it's a ridiculously tasty chick with no combat training. Frankly it probably counts as a holiday miracle every second she hasn't been lured into the back of a van with a plate of cookies and gang-raped to within an inch of her life. It's a good thing her dad is keeping tabs on her through his magical television set, although I'm not so sure it was wise of him to let the head elf know that this is possible. ("I was just looking for the game, Santa! I didn't know she was in the shower!") Beyond this basic setup it's all pretty random: Santa's daughter saves a toy store and a Christmas pageant, and falls in love, while the head elf engages in some underhanded shamfoolery until he finally gets caught less because the good guys did anything proactive and more because it was just about time to wrap things up. Really, Christmas movies don't get much more pointless or insipid than this. They should've at least had the decency to show Santa's daughter naked.

Battle of the Bulbs

(2010)

Max Headroom and the hippie from *C.H.U.D.* play two guys who get into a holiday pissing match over who has the best Christmas decorations. We've all seen this movie before because they make it every year, but despite the fact that it's a pretty solid premise ("People acting like assholes on Christmas") everyone always seems to louse it up. And this might be the worst take yet: it's so forced and fucking obvious, that when the two main guys initiate their feud the word "Peace" on the one dude's "Peace On Earth" sign falls over. The wit! The irritated wives get the only good lines (which numbered almost in the three), Max Headroom's kid looks like what would happen if the Nazis bred the ideal dork, and there's a pointless "fossils in love" sideplot that exists solely to chew up more time, as if this flick isn't a big enough waste of it already. The only redeeming quality is the random, babe-licious housewife who guesses "Ave Maria" during charades at the neighborhood Christmas party. An infinitely better Christmas movie could be made about her and I fucking.

Hey, if she's dressed as an elf and has a candy cane up her ass, it counts as a Christmas movie.

B.C.
A Special Christmas
(1981)

Never mind that, by definition, you can't celebrate Christmas if it's B.C. The real question here is: How will Johnny Hart, the guy who invented *B.C.*, use this cartoon to belittle his many enemies, i.e. every Jew, Muslim, gay person, and non-Presbyterian on the planet? In real life, of course, he just went around sounding off about how they were all gonna burn in Hell, but you can't really get away with that kind of shit in a cartoon special theoretically aimed at kids, so it'll be interesting to see how he sneaks it in here.

The first joke (I guess) is a couple of ants at the ant version of Stonehenge (take that, Druids), but the real story begins when two of the B.C. cavemen decide to write some runes on a slab, bury it, pretend to find it, "translate" it, and then use the yarn they come up with to bamboozle everyone (in your fucking face, Mormons). As part of the con they basically invent Santa Claus, but then it turns out that he was real all along (suck it and die, atheists) so all of their scheming and scamming comes to naught (getting the message, Jews? Now die in Hell).

Welp, looks like Hart definitely got his digs in. The world really is a better place since he croaked.

The Best Present of All
(1992)

"Celebrate the Christmas season with the Donut Man, his pal Duncan, and the Donut Repair Club". Okay, what? For real, why do Christians always have to be so goddamned weird? This is another video that tries to brainwash teach kids about Jesus, although parts of it seem normal enough, like the kids putting on a Christmas show (even if it does sound like they're singing "Joy to the world, the Lord is scum" in one part). And I'll give a pass to the little girl who looks like she has that disease where you die of old age before your 12th birthday. (This video is at least 12 years old, so I guess we won't be seeing any more of her. Her family have requested that any gifts, flowers, and especially cash be sent c/o Mr. Satanism at the address found elsewhere in this book. Seriously, that's what they told me.)

But what the fuck is up with the talking donut? Christians say they hate witchcraft and shit, so why are they always encouraging their kids to hang out with talking animals and satanically-possessed inanimate objects? Talk about sending a mixed message.

At any rate, as far as Christian videos go this isn't particularly obnoxious (mostly they just sing Christmas songs), but it sure pissed somebody off -

the previous owner of my copy tore the main guy's face right off the VHS box. Where's your repair club now, Donut Man? Also, via pencil scribbles, our perp makes it pretty clear that he loves someone named Rachel Chris. Good luck with that, kid.

Black Christmas

(2006)

A new version of *Black Christmas*? Starring Buffy the Vampire Slayer's supafine little sister? Sign me the fuck up. The setup is basically the same – there's sorority chicks, and some cat murders them – but they give the killer entirely too much complicated backstory this time around. He has yellow skin. He saw his dad get murdered. He was locked in the attic for years. He had incest with his mom... Christ, just let the guy be crazy. Also, it doesn't help that he looks a little bit like Mike Myers. The comedian, not the serial killer. Truth be told this whole movie is kind of dumb and sloppy, like it was the first of the month and everybody was loaded on cherry wine when suddenly someone said "Hey! Let's remake *Black Christmas*! You think we can get it out by the 25th?" It is fairly gory though, and the rest of the chicks are pretty in that cookie-cutter Hollywood way that bores the piss out of me but you proles really seem to like. (I did approve of the snarky drunk though; too bad she gets both of her eyes gouged out before we see more of her tits.) As for the plot, it mainly involves people splitting up, but this just means that more of them die horribly which in a movie like this is pretty much the point. They even had the balls to gruesomely off their only big "name", Buffy's sis. Which, as much as I love her, she kinda deserves for ruining Season Five. The end is pretty stupid though. Seriously, so many dead people pop back to life that I thought Jesus was really, finally back and ending up hiding under my bed for several hours.

Bloodbeat

(1982)

It's Christmas, that time of the year when a supernatural samurai warrior rises from the pumpkin patch to run wild in the American heartland, better known as the sticks. But first, some family drama. The hag mom hates her son's new girlfriend! The fine-ass sister (rocking it hard 1980s' style in a t-shirt, panties, and thigh-high legwarmers) (seriously, she looks so fucking fine) has dropped out of school! The girlfriend hates hunting but goes hunting anyway and freaks out! Some walk-on is accidentally shot! Finally the samurai shows up, gorily running people through and downing them with arrows, and accompanied by some serious poltergeist activity wherein one guy is ruthlessly pummeled with dry goods. Through it all, the girlfriend is upstairs, moaning and thrashing around in bed and looking mighty hot doing it if I do say so myself. And I do. So, if I have to venture a guess... the girlfriend is summoning the samurai ghost from Japanese Hell to kill everyone else for shooting Bambi? It's as good an excuse as any, I suppose. I mean, ALL of these Christmas horror movies can't be about a spree killer wearing a Santa suit. There's a fair amount of blood, some middling tits, and it all ends with a mystical showdown à la *Doctor Strange*. The 1970s made-for-TV one, not the one with Benedict Cumberbitch. Much of this showdown is accompanied by "mystical boinging", at least according to the Amazon prime subtitles.

Call Me Claus

(2001)

Is there anyone on Earth who actually likes Whoopi Goldberg? She's so fucking hideous and obnoxious. One time – this is totally true – I worked with this black lady and when some dude tried to mack on her by telling her she looked like Whoopi Goldberg she punched him in the face. It was hilarious. In this movie Santa Claus has to find a replacement ASAP or the North Pole will melt and flood the world (the "Waterworld Clause", one elf calls it), and for some bizarre reason he selects Whoopi Goldberg. It must be a Christmas miracle, because there's actually a couple of cool/funny parts in the early portions of this flick, but mostly it's boring, smarmy, annoying, and stupid. Plus it's completely unrealistic. For example, Whoopi's boss keeps hitting on her, and he isn't even blind. And who would pick her to be Santa Claus anyway? She looks more like the Predator. I know if I thought the fucking Predator was coming down my chimney I'd shoot first and ask questions later, so did the original ever stop to think that maybe she wasn't exactly the best choice for this particular gig? Use your head, Santa. Criminy.

Cancel Christmas

(2010)

The setup is no worse than a million other wretched Xmas flicks (Santa has 30 days to make three angry kids appreciate the joy of giving or Yoko will cancel Christmas), but fuck me did this one go off the rails. Hey, I get that any talentless asswipe, even Justin French, can make a movie these days, but when said movie is actually being shown on a major cable network (okay, fine, the Hallmark Channel) I think I'm well within my rights to expect something a little more professional than this. I mean seriously, I *pay* for cable. Well, most people do, anyway. The whole thing feels like some chintzy film festival movie, the acting reeks of "Who here will work for free?", and Santa's village looks like one of those collectible ceramic Christmas towns your grandma used to set up every year and you inevitably appropriated as a World War Part 2 toy soldier battlefield. (Helpful hint: you can simulate artillery fire with strategically-placed M-80s.)

Did I mention how much the acting sucks? Well it's worth mentioning again. The guy playing Santa is especially bad, but you can tell that he was either completely baked the entire time or just straight-up didn't give a damn and either way it's kind of hard to blame him. Way worse is the infuriating asshat who plays his elf sidekick. Let me tell you, listening to this detestable fuck's laugh is like chewing on tinfoil with your brain. I would murder this shrill, cackling shitstain in front of God, and no matter how many eternal damnations He sentenced me to it would totally be worth it. Getting back to Santa, instead of relying on honesty or Christmas magic (which is *such* a crutch) he achieves his goals primarily through the use of blackmail, but that's nothing compared to the terrible advice this teacher doles out to one kid's dad:

TEACHER: "Remember, Farley wouldn't be so angry if he didn't love you."

Yeah, that's what they said about my cousin's abusive husband too. Hey, Dad, maybe "Farley" is angry because you gave him a dog's name. There's also a brief but highly-appreciated private schoolgirl water fight, a part where the moviemakers are reflected in the side of a car (in the movie biz, not understanding how reflective surfaces work is the number one indicator that you're dealing with bush-league amateurs), and I think the last few minutes are actually a commercial for a wheelchair.

    Dick almighty. If they were gonna cancel anything, it should've been this awful movie.

A Carol Christmas

(2003)

Goddamn it, they've made this "Christmas Carol" shit so many fucking times it's completely pointless. Seriously, do they really think anybody is gonna watch this movie and be all like "Wow, I wonder what will happen?" You'd think with Captain Kirk *and* Arnold from *Diff'rent Strokes* in it it would have to at least be a little hilarious, but Donna from *Beverly Hills 90125* gets the only funny bit when they visit the hood and she says, "Don't tell me we're here to do a Christmas drug deal." Ha ha! I've actually bought drugs on Christmas, so I find that particularly funny. Anyway, this is a total waste of time. The only good thing about it is Donna's ass.

Casper's Haunted Christmas

(2000)

Casper has to scare somebody by Christmas or he'll end up in Hell. Don't do it, Casper! Stick to your guns and maybe we'll never have to read one of your ass-sucking comic books ever again! Also, until he comes through he's banished to "Kriss, Massachusetts", "the most Christmas-y town in the world". Excuse me for a moment.

ARRRRGGGGGHHHHHHHH!!!!!!!!!!!!

Okay. So anyway, Casper and his three ghost uncles start creeping around town getting into shenanigans, but the retarded thing is that *no one notices they're ghosts!* What could possibly look more like a ghost than the fucking ghosts from "Casper"??? How goddamned stupid does this movie think we are??? Seriously, when a movie has the fucking sack to come into MY living room and tell me I'm stupid that's a movie that can SUCK MY FUCKING COCK. There's also tons of piss-awful puns ("It's from the Ghost Office."), a shower scene with a *guy*, and a Slimer clone that does the impossible by being even more irritating than the actual Slimer. And I'm only gonna say this once, you talentless hack fuckholes: *a cartoon can't have bloopers and outtakes*. That was funny the first time somebody did it (well, in theory anyway), but now it's just annoying and yet another insult to my intelligence. If you worked on this miserable piece of garbage you better buy some new locks and stock up on ammo, because rest assured you're on my fucking list.

We do find out one interesting thing in this movie though: Casper was a Boy Scout before he died. I wonder if that's how he got killed? I'll bet he got lost in the woods and eaten by a bear. Or better yet, maybe he was raped and murdered by his Scout Leader, buried in the woods, *then* dug up and eaten by a bear. One can only hope.

A Chipmunk Christmas

(1981)

God damn it, no one on Earth likes the motherfucking Chipmunks and their awful fucking Christmas song. Sure, the stupid cunt sold like gangbusters when it first came out, but that's only because people were buying it as a gag gift to give to other people. No one ever bought a copy of it for *themselves*. The dick who came up with the Chipmunks never figured that out though, so here we are with the Chipmunk Christmas Special. Fuck.

The mind-numbing jackassery begins with this little boy who's dying. That's cheery. Meanwhile, Alvin and the Chipmunks are sucking shit as usual, singing assloads of their idiotic played-at-the-wrong-speed garbage. Fucking disease-carrying bastards. Anyway, Alvin feels bad for the sick kid so he gives him his harmonica, but then, wouldn't you know it, it turns out he needs the bitch for gig so he has to engage in antics to get enough bread to buy a new one. Okay, aren't Alvin and the Chipmunks supposed to be big rock stars or something? And they don't have forty bucks for a top-line harmonica? Seriously, their manager Dave practically shits a brick when he finds out Alvin wants to buy something for himself. What the hell is that asshole doing with all their money? It's probably going up his nose. And apparently he's not the only one with substance abuse problems: that night, Alvin dreams about pink elephants, and we all know what that means. I assume he took a nip right before bed to dull the pain of the coke-fueled off-screen beating he got from Dave for daring to question his handling of the band's finances. In the end the harmonica magically makes the sick kid better (translation: he was faking it) so he shows up at the concert and plays a couple of songs with the Chipmunks while Dave hangs out backstage blatantly macking on his mom and *way* underage sister. Seriously, this girl is like eleven years old, tops. People in the music industry are such fucking degenerates.

Christmas Caper

(2007)

This flick should be flushed down the Christmas *crapper*. Brenda Walsh is a crook who plans to knock over every house on the block while everyone's at the neighborhood Christmas party, but thanks to her annoying, snitchy little niece she discovers the true meaning of Christmas and everybody watching this movie pukes. Fuck, don't they ever get tired of making the exact same Christmas movie over and over again? Just *once* can't they come up with a flick where somebody *doesn't* learn the true meaning of Christmas? Since this movie's completely boring, pointless, and generic anyway they really should've considered going that route. Like for example, instead of giving all the stolen loot back, Brenda could've just kept it. And instead of doing a relatively passable job of taking care of her sister's kids, she could've added to her overall haul by selling them into white slavery. Then at the end when her cop ex-boyfriend gets wise she riddles him with bullets and makes a break for the Mexican border. The last scene would be Brenda in Tijuana, where she does a strip tease out of a sexy Santa outfit to "Jingle Bell Rock", lights up a huge Marley with a fifty dollar bill, and then sits on my face.

You tell me that movie wouldn't rock.

A Christmas Carol
(1984)

Everybody knows this story - they've filmed it like a million times, and any TV show that's on for more than one season always has to have an episode that rips it off because the people who write for TV are as lazy as they fucking come. Just like always, Uncle Scrooge (for some reason he's a person instead of a duck in this version) is a dick to his nephew and the drip who works for him, and doesn't care about Christmas. Everyone else meanwhile is so into it that they border on being deranged. Seriously, when was the last time you invited someone over for holiday dinner and when they said no you gave them like a five minute speech about Christmas? Jesus. Of course on Christmas night the Ghosts of Christmas Past, Christmas Presents, and Christmas Future barge in and give Scrooge the business: the first one takes him back in time to visit his family,* the next ghost (who looks like a cross-dressing lumberjack) shows him how much he pisses everybody off, and finally the GoCF brings it all home by showing Scrooge his own grave. Of course that last bit is what really does the trick - they should've just sent Xmas Future in first and the other two could've taken the night off and grabbed a beer or something.

For all the times I've suffered through it though there's one thing I never understood about this story:

there's plenty of people who are dicks and/or don't like Christmas, so why'd they single this cat out? Or does this eventually happen to everybody? They should make a version where the ghosts run some clown through the wringer but then it turns out he doesn't care about Christmas because he's Jewish. That'd be hilarious.

*His sister's pretty fine - I wouldn't mind getting into her Christmas stockings.

Christmas Comes to Pacland

(1982)

The whole concept that Pac-Man is a real pac that lives in a real place is already completely fucking insane, but when you look at how his society functions in this cartoon it crazies to a whole new level. As I understand it, killer ghosts roam around trying to "chomp" the pac people, which doesn't kill them but does seem to weaken them considerably. The pac people, meanwhile, if they partake of these special pellets, can then eat the ghosts. But when they eat the ghosts it's only temporary and the ghosts "get better" after a while, which leads me to believe that they really are disembodied spirits. Okay, here's my theory: after a given number of attacks, the pac people DO die, and the ghosts are actually the spirits of dead pac people! It all fits. Hell, in this very cartoon one ghost says of Pac-Man, "Come on, let's quit wasting time and chomp on his bones!"

It turns out the concept frightens Santa's reindeer as well, because when a bunch of disembodied ghost eyes go flying by his sleigh they panic and Santa crashes. (Do you think when Santa works out his schedule each year he takes into account that he's going to have at least one misadventure along the way? He ought to.) (Regardless, the pac people, it seems, are godless pagans who have never heard of Christmas. Maybe all the extant pac-ghosts were originally sacrifices to their powerful and almost certainly evil pagan god.) Anyway, Santa loses his toys in the crash, but they eventually turn up and Xmas is saved, although I noticed that he only has eight reindeer here and since one of them is Rudolph I assume that means that one of the originals died. I hope it was Donner. I never liked that Donner.

Incidentally, and I can't believe Pac-Man is shown to own a pac-dog and a pac-cat, but no pac-rat. I mean really, that gag is kind of a no-brainer.

Christmas Do-Over

(2006)

This guy doesn't want to spend Christmas with his ex-family (duh), but he has no choice because a big boulder falls into the road and traps him in town. (Where the fuck do these people live? The Smurf village?) Of course his ex-in-laws all hate him, and his ex-wife has a boyfriend now who's utterly perfect and asks her to marry him. His kid is still happy to see him though and wishes it was Christmas every day, so since wishes made by little kids always come true (except of course mine, when I wished that daddy would stop hitting me), everything goes all *Groundhog Day* on the guy and Christmas keeps happening over & over. The main guy does do some hilarious shit, like getting into a fistfight with Jesus, but of course it all ends with him learning the true spirit of blah blah blah and getting back together with his ex. I don't know what happens to her perfectly nice new boyfriend after she drops him like a bad habit, on Christmas, just as he was about to propose to her. Maybe he kills himself.

Christmas Every Day
(1996)

Confession time: I secretly love these movies where someone has to relive the same day over & over again. I know it's because they're supposed to learn some queer lesson or something, but if it ever happens to me you can rest assured that I won't learn squat. I mean seriously, what sounds better: learning a valuable lesson, or living forever and doing whatever you want with absolutely no consequences? I thought so. Unfortunately, the kid in this movie barely takes advantage of it at all - he doesn't even start any fires! Talk about a lack of imagination. I mean come on, it all resets anyway so that means you could be as degenerate as you wanted and it wouldn't matter because the next day it *literally never happened*. At the very least he should've tried to get a little play off his cousin; she's about his age and she's really fucking cute. Yeah, yeah, I know, you're not supposed to do that, but obviously you aren't listening to what I just said: she's *really* fucking cute.

Christmas Evil

(1980)

This dude watched Santa Claus feel up his mom when he was little (it's like a novelty song gone all wrong), so now he spies on all the kids in the neighborhood and keeps these lists re: who's good and who's bad. Honestly, I really don't see the connection, but whatever. When Christmas rolls around he goes off the deep end, dresses up as Santa, steals all these toys and delivers them to the good kids. Plus he kills a couple of people just to keep things interesting. Eventually some people track him down and a huge torch-waving mob forms and starts chasing the dude.* It looks like it's curtains for him, but he makes it to his van and as he flees the fan takes flight and disappears into the sky because apparently he was the real Santa Claus all along! If you ask me there weren't anywhere near enough murders in this movie, but I gotta give 'em credit - that ending's sure to piss off damn near everyone, which makes it pretty awesome.

*Where do you even *buy* torches, especially on Christmas Eve?

The Christmas Gift
(1986)

John Denver visits this podunk town to see if it would be a good place to build condos, and discovers that everybody there – even the grownups – believes in Santa Claus. For those of you who don't remember John Denver, he was basically a combination of a country music singer and a nerd. His big shtick was guest-starring on every single TV show that came out in the 1970s, and he was actually pretty popular until he died of crashing his airplane into the ocean. And I want to take a moment here to make it absolutely clear that I was in no way, shape, or form doing bong hits with him behind the aircraft maintenance building right before it happened. I wasn't anywhere *near* Monterey that day - I was in Cleveland.

Anyway, back to the movie. John Denver figures they're all cracked (which they are), but he falls in love with the mom from *Malcolm in the Middle* (wow, she was ugly back then too) so he decides to stick around, stab his boss in the back, and help them save Red Foreman's ranch. That's right, not only do they save Christmas in this movie, they save a ranch too. How fucking gay. By which I mean heartwarming. By which I mean gay.

A Christmas Horror Story

(2015)

A slick, entirely Christmas-themed horror anthology featuring William Shatner? I've died and gone to niche genre heaven. Admittedly, this movie isn't the best example of any of those things, but there are a couple of good jump scares, moderate gore, and a couple of exceptionally hot teenage girls. Three kids are trapped in a high school basement with the ghost of Christmas pissed; an obnoxious family is stalked by an albino Krampus; a little boy is swapped out for a changeling, resulting in A Very Bad Seed Christmas; and, in the dumbest story, Santa himself throws down with a horde of foul-mouthed zombie elves (this last one does have a good twist ending, at least). In between, Shatner makes like the DJ in *The Warriors* with a bunch of rambling but entertaining nonsense. There's no tits or sacrilege, which knocks it down a couple of pegs, but other than that it's reasonably solid holiday horror.

Christmas in July

(1940)

It astounds me that retailers still haven't jumped all over the "Christmas in July" concept. I mean, these circus clowns insist that they operate at a loss ten months out of the year, so you'd think they'd be ecstatic to get a secondary Christmas up and running. Of course, if you operate at a loss ten months out of the year it's pretty obvious that you don't know shit about running a business, so I guess it's not surprising that they haven't figured this out yet.

So, Maxford House Coffee ("Grand to the Last Gulp!") is having a contest, and the office cutups trick our main guy into thinking that he won first prize, $25,000. You figure he'll look quite the fuckhead when he shows up to get his check, but as it turns out the boss over at Maxford House hates contests ("All they prove is that you're making too much money in the first place, since you can afford to toss a large chunk to some saphead..."), so he isn't paying a fuck bit of attention to what's going on and just turns the bread over, which means that our boy really does wind up with 25,000 smackers. Now by my estimation that's about 10 call girls, depending on how you tip, but he has other plans. First he calls his mom and tells her they're rich, then he goes on an out-of-control shopping spree that includes an engagement ring (the fool), a futuristic couch, toys, a fur coat, and presents for everyone in the neighborhood. Mom, meanwhile, assumes he's delusional ("I know. My Irving, he drinks too," one old bat commiserates), until he shows up with all the swag and starts handing it out like stale candy the week after Halloween. I'm sure you can see where this is going, and you're right: fraud and grand theft charges. There's almost a riot first though, which would've been awesome and I'm really sorry they didn't got that route. Nevertheless, this flick is actually reasonably intelligent for a movie with such a misunderstanding-oriented setup, and as such it's one of the few non-horror movies in this book that I'm going to give my Mr. Satanism Seal of Approval™. Spoiler warning.

Christmas in July

(1979)

This is like the ultimate puppet-toon movie: Rudolph the Red-Nosed Reindeer, Frosty the Snowman, Jack Frost, *and* Santa Claus are in it! The bad guy is this evil wizard who has a magic scepter of "solid ice" (what other kind of ice is there?), and he tries to defeat the lot of them with a ridiculously convoluted plan involving a circus, magic amulets, mind control, a tornado, an evil reindeer, rein*snakes*, a fake cop, and Ethyl Merman riding a giraffe. It's fucking insane. Frankly though I think they should've taken it even further: can you imagine if they threw in the Little Drummer Boy, Nestor the Donkey, Peter Cottontail, Baby New Year, the fucking Christmas leprechauns, and that weird-ass Earth-2 Santa who was raised by the lion and shit? It'd be like the *Crisis on Infinite Earths* of puppet-toons, and would probably be only slightly more incomprehensible.

Seriously, they need to get crackin'. I'd pay good cash money to see that.

The Christmas List
(1997)

This chick actually puts some effort into her crappy customer service job, which is movie shorthand for "she's nice". Or, as this one kid puts it, "It's like you really care about stuff." You can't be more vague than that. One day she makes a joke list of all the shit she wants for Christmas, but when her hot-ass best friend throws it into this department store Santa's mailbox a Christmas miracle occurs and everything on the list starts to appear! (Never mind that someone else has to get shafted for some of the wishes to materialize; this movie isn't about those people.) When the main chick gloms what's going down she makes another list, and what do you think she asks for:

A) World peace
B) An over-the-counter cure for syphilis
C) Food for all the starving children in the universe
D) Makeup and an engagement ring

Well, she is a woman so I think you know the answer. By the time the magic Santa dust finally clears she's fraudulently won a car, stolen another broad's boyfriend, and turned her own mother into a Christmas pod person. Meanwhile I've still got the syfy. Fucking weak.

Christmas on Chestnut Street
(2006)

There's a big Christmas decorating contest, and the main guy in this movie gets roped into it even though his dad has senile dementia (don't worry, it's mostly the hilarious kind) and just wants an old-fashioned Christmas. Naturally the whole thing gets completely out of hand, until finally the dad flips out, trashes his front yard, and everyone learns a valuable lesson: old people belong in homes. This could have been an okay flick, but unfortunately most of it is about the main guy falling in love with this hot redhead. Now don't get me wrong, if I was him I'd be trying to get down her chimney too, but I was expecting shitloads of fighting, sabotage, and wholesale destruction and all we get is a single deflated snowman balloon and one lousy brawl. Seriously people, you're involved in a *contest;* is this really the best you can do? Needless to say this whole movie, and almost everyone in it, is pretty fucking lame. I did like the scheming Jewish broad, but my profile at match.com does say "Seeks scheming Jew" so that shouldn't come as any big surprise.

Christmas on Mars

(2008)

The first time we see the main guy in this movie he's moping around because he killed some moths when he was a kid. "I don't know why I did it," he thinks. Dude, they eat your fucking clothes - you did the right thing. Write an entry about it on your blog if you must and then get over it, pussy. Anyway, he works on a space station and all he wants to do is throw a Christmas party for everybody, but this is complicated by the fact that the place is falling apart and they're all gonna die. Also people keep hallucinating, and an alien shows up. It's all surprising interesting and fairly freaky... until we see the goofball alien, which is just some guy in a bad costume. I think the cat in charge says it best: "What the fuck is this faggot up to?" For real, he looks like a cross between Mork from Ork and the cover of Ringo Starr's *Goodnight Vienna*. They should've just had him look like a normal guy - almost everyone thinks he's just one of the other astronauts wearing a stupid costume anyway, so it's not like it would mess up the plot. Plus if his ultimate identity was all mysterious and shit the viewer could draw their own conclusions and that would ultimately make this movie seem a lot more clever than it actually is. It's still an okay flick though, and you should definitely check it out. It is pretty pretentious how much it wants to be *Solaris* (you can tell because it has Russian subtitles but not any other kind), but it also has a scene where a baby gets trampled to death by a marching band with vagina heads, so I'd say that balances things out.

The Christmas Season Massacre

(2001)

Here's another piece of shit. A white trash guy sporting an eye patch goes around killing these retards who made fun of him for having only one shoe. You know, people leave shoes lying by the side of the road all the time - if it was that big of a deal to him, why didn't he just pick one of them up? It wouldn't make for much of a movie, but it's definitely a more straightforward solution to his problem. Some chicks show off their tits, but since the main reason the killer's able to catch most of them is because they're too fat to run away it's that's definitely not a good thing. The only interesting parts are when the cutest chick (by default) gets stabbed in the pussy, and when one guy nails his (fat, hideous) girl while wearing a cardboard watermelon on his head because, really, how often are you going to see that? And what does any of this have to do with Christmas? They *say* it's all taking place during Christmas, but there's no snow or Santa Claus or fingering your girlfriend under the table during Christmas dinner while her dad's going on and on about your "plans for his daughter" or anything. *Die Hard* takes place during Christmas, but they didn't call it "Die Hard...on *Christmas*". (Besides, I'm pretty sure they're saving that for Part IX.) So in addition to sucking, this movie is totally dishonest. The credits do inform us that it was made in Missouri though, so as far as I'm concerned that explains everything.

Christmas Vacation 2: Cousin Eddie's Island Adventure

(2003)

Everyone knows the original three Vacation movies: *Vacation* (1983), *European Vacation* (1985), and *Christmas Vacation* (1989), and most of you are probably aware that there was a fourth one, *Vegas Vacation* (1997). But did you know that there was *another* fourth one? That's right, there's a goddamned *Christmas Vacation 2*, even though *Christmas Vacation* was *Vacation Part 3*, which means that this sequel is somehow going *backwards* and will eventually be followed by *Christmas Vacation 1*, *Christmas Vacation 0*, and then several negatively-numbered installments until everyone is so confused that they just start naming them after the year they take place, just like "Christmas '59", the short story *Christmas Vacation/Vacation 3* was based on in the first place. And you thought calling the fourth one **The** *Final Destination* was confusing.

So, unfortunately for us, but fortunately for the cast and crew (because in real life he's quite the dick), Clark Griswold isn't even in this Vacation movie. Instead, it focuses on Cousin Eddie, who's funny in small doses but can carry an entire movie about as effectively as my high school girlfriend carried any of her pregnancies to term. Backing him up are his wife, another one of their kids that we've never seen before, and the original Audrey, arguably the finest of the four Audreys who have appeared in this franchise so far. (Seriously, how goddamned convoluted is the *Vacation* continuity, anyway? It's worse than fucking Marvel Comics.) Oh, and Lou Grant. For some reason, Lou Grant is along for the ride. Did you know that he's a 9/11 "Truther"? Fuck Lou Grant.

Like the actor who plays Cousin Eddie himself, everything about this movie is obvious and annoying: it consists almost entirely of falling down and farting, and I swear, they say "Christmas vacation" so many times that it could be a drinking game. Maybe the producers were afraid that, since the story mostly takes place on a tropical island and doesn't even feature the series' main character, people would forget what the hell they were even watching and have to be constantly reminded, which come to think of it is probably a pretty astute assumption. Limited highlights include Audrey in tight pants, Audrey sunbathing, Audrey's infectious smile, and Audrey's Maxim photo shoot that I found online after this awful movie was over. I love you, Audrey #1. I love you.

Dammit, I see another restraining order in my near future.

The Christmas Wife
(1988)

Max Dugan wants his family to come home for the holidays, but since there's four of them and only one of him they think *he* should come visit *them*. He's so fucking stubborn though that he totally refuses and pays an *escort company* to hook him up instead! Now that might make sense if he was trying to get some yuletide action, but he just wants someone to spend Christmas with, as long as it isn't his family because they won't do things his way. Boomers gotta boom. The rest of the movie consists of Max and the flaky old bag the escort service dug up* having the dullest conversation in the history of the world until it *finally* decides to end which I'm pretty sure was at least 18 hours later. It did seem like something interesting (if gross) was gonna happen when Max talked about playing with his "tiffle" (Old Bag: "Your tiffle? I'd like to see that."), but it turns out a "tiffle" just a ukulele. This flick really is the worst ever; being in solitary confinement is probably less boring. I honestly can't believe I got through it without killing myself.

*I don't mean "dug up" literally, but from the looks of her it won't be very long.

A Colbert Christmas
The Greatest Gift of All!
(2008)

Back in the 1970s and 1980s they used to pummel us with special Christmas episodes and episodic Christmas specials all the time, even though hardly any of them were ever any good. I think there was a *Diff'rent Strokes* one where we saw Kimberly's tits, but that's about it. I guess Colbert Report is trying to poke fun at those types of specials with this program, but unfortunately he forgot to make it not a boring piece of crap. I find this very hard to understand - why is it he could be funny five nights a week on his regular program, but he can't pull it off for one Xmas special? I'd say "nice try" but that would be a lie because *he doesn't try at all*. Seriously, Willie Nelson sings about pot? Is it even possible to measure time in small enough increments to explain how long it took to come up with *that?* The only good parts are: the Toby Keith song; Feist dressed as an angel singing a joke version of "Angels We have Heard on High" that was dumb but still made me want to come to Bethlehem and see, not to mention all over her face;* and Santa fighting a bear.

By the way, Colbert, all the "jokes" about over-pimping the DVD of your crappy Christmas Special stop being jokes – and therefore stop being funny –

when there really is a DVD of your crappy Christmas Special for sale. I'm gonna give you a pass this time because you're usually awesome, but next time I better see a vast improvement or it's into the "fad" locker with you. I'm sure we can find some room right between Shaboozey and those worthless Pabst-swiller magnets Vampire Weekend.

*Don't think Feist is hot? You're gay.

A Collection of Christmas Classics
(2006)

In this case, of course, "classic" means "old enough to use for free". This tape is over four hours long, so it would be the perfect thing to keep the rugrats out of your hair if it wasn't so fucking lame that even little kids won't want to watch it. Here's what's on it:

Rudolph the Red-Nosed Reindeer (1944) This version takes place in some fucked-up surreal reindeer land where reindeer wear clothes, live in houses (when Santa discovers Rudolph, Rudolph's sleeping in bed), and climb trees. Jesus, can you imagine if deer could climb trees in real life? How would you get away from one that was trying to eat you then?

The Snow Queen (1957) All these kids want Art Linkletter to read them *The Snow Queen*, but he convinces them to watch the movie instead. Lazy fuck. Anyway, the Snow Queen (she looks like She-Ra's frigid half-sister) gets pissed when this kid disses her, so she kidnaps him and freezes his heart. His girl comes looking for him, but she ends up getting kidnapped by a *different* witch who steals her memory, and after she escapes she's kidnapped *again* by a crazy, knife-wielding dyke. What is wrong with these kids? At any rate she eventually locates her boo and then everything just magically fixes itself – with no effort on anyone's part whatsoever – by falling out of the writer's ass. Weak.

Santa and the Three Bears (1970) I review this bizarre shit later in this book.

The Little Christmas Burro (1978) Ditto

The Alpha-Bots Christmas (2004) As Superman once said, "Welcome to the bottom of the barrel." This piece of fucking crap would make even the biggest Pollyanna Christmas lover shit themselves with fury. Basically it's an endless parade of these awful cartoon-effect robots flying around doing absolutely nothing. There's 26 of them ("A-Bot", "B-Bot", "C-Bot", etc.), they're all different, and they make damn sure we get a good look at each and every one of the bastards. In fact, in one part they all introduce themselves, one at a time. It's fucking infuriating and...

Okay, hold up. I think I see what's going on here, so let me clear something up for these pinheads: *No one is going to make a toy line out of your awful fucking cartoon.* Even if they did (proving, as a corollary, that there is no God), obviously anyone who got an "Alpha-Bot" would immediately be reminded of the video and would get so angry that they would smash the damn thing with a rock. In fact, I think most people would be so pissed off that they wouldn't even take the time to go outside and find a rock, they'd probably just throw it at the nearest wall or possibly flip out completely and try to eat the fucking thing. And then "Alpha-Bots LLC" would have a class-action lawsuit on its hands. Which would be awesome.

Christmas Comes But Once a Year (1936) After the Alpha-Bots (may they rust in hell forever) anything would look good, even this awful cartoon about a bunch of orphans and their shitty Christmas. Actually the part where all their cheap toys fall apart and they cry is pretty hilarious. Sorry, orphans, but in this life some of us are winners, and some of us are...you.

Snow Foolin' (1949) This is one of those old-timey cartoons where there's no story as such, just a bunch of dumb "gags" that completely suck. It's fucking garbage. Buy War Bonds.

The Shanty Where Santy Claus Lives (1933) Another super-old cartoon (it's in black & white), but at least this one's racist. The "Sambo Jazz Band"? Ha ha!

Okay, the box says that the puppet-toon *Jack Frost* is next (you know, the one where he asks Father Winter to make him human so he can score some ass), but it's not on here! Instead there's six more shitty old cartoons, and some of them don't even have anything to do with Christmas! *Motherfuckers.* These cartoons are weird, too: in one, this homeless guy takes off his shirt and he's sporting a bra *and* an NRA tattoo, and in another one instead of cookies & milk Santa gets a pastry, a bottle of wine, a cigar, and a hard-boiled egg. Fucking French.

Cranberry Christmas

(2008)

What the ass is this shit? This isn't a Christmas special, it's a insultingly transparent ad for cranberries, AKA fruit's armpit. And not only will they not shut up about the fucking cranberries, but they also slander the competition by naming the bad guy "Mr. Grape". The story, such as it is, concerns a minor property dispute, always a subject that will keep young children glued to the edge of their seats. Here are some actual scenes from this thrilling Christmas special:

- A guy examining some legal documents
- A fat lady writing a letter to her brother
- An old man sleeping

Ethel Merman riding a flying giraffe is looking pretty good at this point. There is one decent part where the bad guy breaks into someone's house and completely trashes the place, but other than that it's boring beyond words. Maybe they were afraid that anything more exciting would get in the way of their simple, timeless holiday message: Buy more cranberries. What a load of fucking garbage. Fuck you Ocean Spray; go peddle you shit to someone who cares. Which is nobody.

Cricket on the Hearth
(1967)

This is introduced by a real guy, who seems pretty confused (read: drunk). The actual cartoon portion begins with a cricket letting himself in through a window to get out of a snowstorm. What the fuck? Did he just say "It's a *shitty* one"??? Anyway, the cricket tells the main story, which, naturally, is full of gratuitous animals and songs that suck absolute shit. The number one problem with this cartoon though is that the cricket *looks like a penis*. No matter what was happening onscreen, I just sat there thinking to myself "I'm watching a penis save Christmas". If it was that distracting for me, I can't imagine how a girl could watch this. And what does the singing cat have to do with anything? And why does the bad guy send his pet crow to a bar to hire a monkey to kill the cricket? Doesn't he own any shoes? (I did like how this little scheme played out though: the monkey, the crow, and their cat partner decide to kidnap the cricket instead so they can sell him to this sea captain, but instead of paying up the sea captain pulls out a handgun and *shoots and kills all three of them*.) And really, wasn't this cartoon weird and dumb enough without having a bunch of toys come to life and then do absolutely nothing? Seriously, this is completely nonsensical and horrible beyond belief. Fuck you, Charles Dickens.

Deck the Halls
(2006)

Christmas movies almost always suck ass, but in the first few minutes of this one there's a meth joke and a mutilated cat joke so it seems like it might be okay. Too bad they screw it all up. Ferris Bueller is this uptight guy who gets into a feud with his obnoxious neighbor over Christmas lights. You would think that this would lead to some Christmas hilarity (you know, arguments, fistfights, etc.) but unfortunately there's just not that many funny parts. When you can't think of enough jokes, destroying shit is always your next best option, but there's nowhere near enough of that either. The obnoxious guy does have some trampy twin daughters, and Ferris Bueller's daughter has some pretty impressive twins of her own, but we never see any of these chicks in all their Christmas glory so even that doesn't help. Seriously, the least they could've done was have it end with both guy's houses being utterly destroyed while their daughters rolled around in the snow having a three-way catfight that turns into a dyke fest. Don't they owe us that much? I mean come on, it *is* fucking Christmas.

A Dennis the Menace Christmas
(2007)

This opens in outer space, then we zoom down, down, down to Santa's house at the North Pole. Then it turns out Santa's house is actually inside a snow globe, and *then* it turns out the whole thing is just a dream! For Christ's sake, it's a Dennis the Menace movie - what the hell is going on? And it doesn't stop not making sense here: next we see Dennis the Menace in a Thanksgiving play, but he lets this turkey out of its cage and then all the other kids suddenly start a food fight for *absolutely no reason*. Later Mr. Wilson flips out on Dennis the Menace's parents and says he never wants their kid on his property again but two seconds later he's babysitting him, and in the end Dennis the Menace is rewarded with accolades and a bike for causing $45,000 worth of damage to Mr. Wilson's house and almost killing the man (twice). Seriously, nothing that happens in this movie has any connection to anything else that happens - it's like the laws of causality do not apply to *A Dennis the Menace Christmas*.

Since there's no logical progression of anything, I'll just list some of the stuff that happens:

- Dennis the Menace gets Mr. Wilson's name in a "secret Santa" drawing
- Mr. Wilson reveals that he is a Marxist
- We learn that, in the world of Dennis the Menace, "stupid" is a cuss word
- Dennis the Menace is accused of sexual assault
- A black guy from outer space gets stuck in Mr. Wilson's chimney
- Mr. Wilson travels through time
- The Olsen Twins are elected President

I swear to fucking God I'm not making any of this up - it's one of the most surreal things I've ever seen in my entire goddamn life, and I'm older than your parents. If you plan on being on drugs any time between now and Christmas, you HAVE to watch this movie. In fact, for people who do drugs this will probably become like a holiday staple.

Bonus: Dennis the Menace's mom has a fantastic ass.

Don't Open Till Christmas
(1984)

This rotter catches Santa getting some so naturally, years later, he goes crazy and starts killing every Santa he sees. (Why *Seeing Santa Get Laid = Become a Slasher Killer* is a trope I have no idea, but rest assured it's an established trope.) Our killer doesn't fuck around, either - in one scene he just marches up to a drunken Santa and sticks a gun right in his mouth. Blam! Happy holidays, dickhead. There's a chick in a Santa suit and thigh-high boots who shows us her tits, an insanely hot stripper in a leather skirt who doesn't (she's a *stripper* - that's total bullshit), and tons of cool, fucked-up murders. If you only have time to watch a three or four Christmas slasher movies this holiday season, make sure this one is on the list.

Elves
(1989)

Three dumb chicks accidentally raise evil Xmas elves, originally the result of a fiendish – by which I mean ridiculous, obviously – experiment by those villainous mainstays, the Nazis. (Cf. *The Little People* by John Christopher.) After some mild preliminary terrorizing the elves invade a local shopping mall, where they square off with Grizzly Adams and the three bimbos before fleeing into the night. Later the elves and their semi-competent Nazi masters track the main chick down for a little rape so that they can sire (what else?) the Nazi/elf Antichrist! Clearly this is enough top-notch insanity for any movie, but this flick really piles it on by being delightfully tasteless and mean-spirited throughout. A little kid spies on his own sister in the shower; a woman drowns a cat in the toilet; a mall Santa feels up a girl sitting on his lap and then does cocaine; the main chick learns, on Christmas Eve, that her grandfather is also her father (You know how some families open one present each on Christmas Eve? I wonder if that counts as hers?); and nearly everyone we meet seems to be miserable, a dick, or both. So yeah, despite some minor flaws (the elves don't wreak anywhere near enough havoc; the cutest chick dies first), this one is definitely a keeper.

Ernest Saves Christmas

(1988)

There's a whole bunch of these Ernest movies (*Ernest Saves Christmas*; *Ernest Saves Camp*; *Ernest Saves Jail*; *Ernest Saves Face*; *Earnest Saves on Car Insurance*), but I never bothered watching any of them before now because let's face it, I'm angry enough as it is. As it turns out though, this one, at least, is fairly tolerable. Santa Claus is looking for his replacement, and in most movies his pick would be the star, no matter how inappropriate, annoying, or repugnant that choice would actually be. In this case though the guy he has his eye on makes perfect sense, but before he can pass the torch a bunch of circumstances go awry and Santa winds up in the slammer. You know, Santa Claus ends up in jail in a lot of Christmas flicks, and I can't help but wonder if this is supposed to be a parallel to that other Christmas guy. One of these days I'd like to see a movie follow through on this angle and actually show Santa getting tried, convicted, and crucified. Then he could rise from the dead and found his own religion: "Santa-ria".

Anyway, back to Ernest. Before Santa gets arrested he leaves his magic bag in Ernest's's's cab,* so Ernest ends up tracking him down and lending a hand, along with this farm-fresh little hottie who looks like Punky Brewster's delinquent older sister. (This chickie dresses as a schoolgirl at one point, and trust me when I tell you that this movie is almost worth watching for that alone. Although her skirt could've been a lot shorter.) It's your typical Xmas crap, and I wouldn't recommend it to someone I was trying to impress or anything, but not unlike *The Fast and the Furious 3* it's probably the best possible *Ernest Saves Christmas* that could theoretically exist. Hell, they even wrap it all up with the freshly-retired Santa landing himself some Bobtail! The only truly painful part is the sideplot concerning these two warehouse guys who have to deal with Santa's reindeer. Every time they broke out that dumb rattling sound effect to underscore the fat guy's eyes moving back and forth I wanted to knock someone's Christmas teeth out.

*Fuck you. You try pronouncing the possessive form of "Ernest".

Eve's Christmas

(2004)

The chick in this movie is fully independent and successful and whatnot, so it looks like it's time for a Christmas miracle to bring a man into her life so she can forget all that nonsense, cook me some dinner, and start popping out babies. She decides to wish on a Christmas star, and I'll be fucked Muslim style if it doesn't work and she ends up going back in time to when she almost got married. This time she decides to go through with it, plus she makes some other changes, like hooking up her best friend so she can get hitched too. Movies regularly act like getting married is the ultimate happy ending, but they always seem to forget that afterwards you have to BE married. And what about *my* Christmas wish, to see the best friend naked? She's pretty cute but her suckle sacks don't make a single appearance.

These goddamn Christmas movies almost never have tits in them. It's gonna be a long month.

A Family Circus Christmas
(1979)

This is some seriously fucked-up shit, and it ended up rocking about a hundred times harder then I ever thought it would. It starts out with the Family Circus kids getting ready for Christmas and being super annoying, just like in their lame-ass newspaper comic, but then Jeffy gets so excited he loses his mind or something, because he starts experiencing these hallucinations in which Santa Claus is stalking him and judging him and shit. Later he decides he wants Santa to, I swear to fucking God, *bring his dead grandpa back to life*. I presumed this was all building up to him learning a valuable lesson about death (pretty heavy for a Christmas cartoon, but not too outside the box), but then the dead grandpa really *does* come back, as a ghost! Leave it to the Family Circus to totally miss the point and scare the absolute shit out of little kids on Christmas. I wish they still showed this on TV every year.

A Family Thanksgiving

(2010)

The main chick in this movie is a strong, independent, career-minded single woman who doesn't want to spend her life comparison shopping for toilet brushes and hosting PTA bake sales in the suburbs. And you know what that means: she needs to get brain-raped with the true meaning of ~~Christmas~~ Thanksgiving. And if it brings her down a few pegs, all the better, the uppity bitch. So what happens? Well, she hits her head and wakes up in an alternate reality/complex hallucination where she's married with two kids. At first she's hatin' it,* but eventually she learns to suppress her own personality and fully dedicate herself to the demands of her empty-headed husband and vile, thankless offspring. Unlike you she does eventually wake up from this nightmare, but by that point she's learned her lesson: a woman's place is in the home. Of course back in the real world she still has this pesky legal career to deal with, but that's easily taken care of: she just strolls into the courtroom and blatantly throws her client's case! Fuck ethics, it's time to have some babies!

*Who wouldn't? And don't lie, actual parents, we all know you'd strangle them in their sleep if you could.

For Better or For Worse
Home for the Holidays
(1992)

Frankly, seeing the *For Better or For Worse* people come to life was a little disturbing, but at least they weren't constantly shedding dirt and dandruff like in their comic strip, and the first cartoon episode on this tape did get off to a hilarious start with Michael saying that all women are dumb and have fat asses. Unfortunately, the actual story begins with a broken Christmas tree angel. The infinitely more fucked-up *Family Circus* Xmas cartoon was about a missing Christmas tree star (well, that and raising the dead). Do people really get that attached to Christmas tree ornaments? At any rate, later Elizabeth (one of the FBoFW kids, if you're too young to remember this comic) gets a concussion and meets this deranged old woman who teaches her a valuable lesson that I didn't quite catch because the sound is so shitty that you can't understand a goddamn thing she's saying. I think she told Elizabeth to stay outta Compton and then compared her to a sandwich.

The second episode is about Halloween, and it's way more entertaining. This time everyone goes to a fall carnival, where they gamble and steal. Also Michael almost gets into a brawl and the family dog goes apeshit and trashes the place. (Fucking

Pattersons. You can't take them anywhere.) We also learn that Michael listens to a band called "Dead Yuppie" and has a "no women" sign on the inside of his bedroom door. Since he's a teenager, I can only assume that this is a clue to his sexual orientation. The best part though is when Michael and his friends go trick-or-treating; instead of a costume, one of his cronies just wears a beer hat so he can walk around the neighborhood getting loaded.

I love Canadians. Even their kids are drunks.

Fred Claus

(2007)

Why anyone decided to throw Hollywood actually-see-it-in-a-theater money at a made-for-the-Family Channel movie like this is beyond me. Basically, Santa has an older brother who hates him and is a huge slack-ass, but of course when the chips are down he rises to the cliché and saves Christmas. And even though Santa's assistant (serving as the main chick) is a delectable blonde babe he's *not* doing it, even in part, because he's in love with her and/or wants to impress his way into her pants. Hell, I'd save *two* Christmases and half a Ramadan for a chance to lick some holiday frosting off that. At any rate this flick is way too long, and in one part it features the worst Christmas song of all time ("Christmas Wrapping") by one of the worst bands in history (the Waitresses), but every once in a while it deteriorates into complete slapstick violence and those parts are reasonably funny. On the puke-o-meter it topped off at just under two liters, well within the normal range for an Xmas movie. If you need a sense of how that translates into real numbers, waking up next to the lead singer of the Waitresses (when she was still alive; let's not be gross here) had a puke-o-meter rating of about six gallons. Seven if you ate her out first.

Frosty's Winter Wonderland
(1976)

Frosty the Snowman comes around for a visit, but he gets lonely and I guess some of the kids he hangs with caught *Bride of Frankenstein* on the late show or something because they decide to build him a snow wife.* Then they build a snow minister to marry them. You know, it's not hard to imagine this spiraling out of control pretty quickly; like that incident with Calvin, Hobbes, and the snow goons, except a million times worse. Jack Frost is on humanity's side at first; he wants to murder Frosty! But he lets himself get sweet-talked out of killing so it's just pure luck that we all didn't end up living in a nightmarish hellscape ruled by inhuman homunculi. Thank god for global warming.

---

*For some reason he requests a fat chick. Just what the world needs, another fat chick. Thanks, Frosty.

The Glo Friends Save Christmas
(1985)

You know, everyone in these cartoons is always "saving" Christmas, but has anyone, even once, ever had to actually do that? Sure, sometimes you don't get anything but socks, or your dad comes home drunk and throws the tree through the picture window because he found out where mommy was *really* spending her Saturday afternoons, but Christmas still *happens*. And how come nobody ever has to save Pearl Harbor Day, or National Library Week, or even Easter? You could probably create a whole new subgenre of cartoon characters saving second- or even third-rate holidays. Why am I always the one who has to suggest this stuff?

So anyway, this time it's the Wicked Witch of the North Pole causing all the trouble. (I can't believe this broad couldn't find a better place to be the Wicked Witch of. There's *nothing* up there. Hell, even the Wicked Witch of Taco Bell probably gets free drink refills.) She traps Santa and his reindeer in an ice cage, so it's up to the Glo Friends to save the day. (For those of you who don't remember the 1980s, "Glo Friends" were these ~~popular~~ toy bugs that glowed in the dark.) You'd think the witch would just step on them and that would be the end of that, but for some reason she never thinks of this and the Glo Friends manage to melt the ice cage and Christmas is saved. Santa gives the Glo Friends their gift in a big bag (we never actually see what it is but I'm guessing it's dog shit - bugs love dog shit) and then he's off to bring joy to all the children of the world (except of course the Jews). The witch, I assume, just goes back to whatever it is she does the other 364 days a years she's not trying to ruin Christmas, which probably involves watching a lot of daytime TV. That Taco Bell gig probably looks pretty good around mid-July or so.

At first I couldn't figure out why anybody would even make this special when there were any number of more popular toys circa 1985 that could've saved Christmas (G.I. Joe would've handed that witch her ass, for example), but I looked it up and it turns out there was actually a proper Glo Friends series back then that I was apparently too not gay to ever watch. If you were into it though, the Internet Movie Database also recommends *The Amazing Race*.

Grandma Got Run Over by a Reindeer

(2000)

I don't care what anyone says, this is an awesome song. Think about it: it's about some liquored-up old bat *literally* getting killed by Santa Claus, and how her husband hated her so fucking much that he considers her death a Christmas present to him. That's some undeniably hilarious shit. (Alternately, the husband did it and it just using Santa Claus as an alibi, which might be even better.) Why they would make a cartoon of it twenty years after it was released is beyond me, but what's even more baffling is why they felt the need to fuck it all up. First off, grandma doesn't even die! That's like making a Jaws movie with no shark. Also she's not a drunk; instead, they say she's allergic to eggs! Really, could this be any more pussified??? I mean, what the Christ-kicking fuck??? Why even make this if you're just gonna piss it all up? *Why, why, why???* It's just a bunch of cutesy bullshit, and it's not like there's a fucking shortage of that around Christmas. Since this cartoon refuses to actually be about what's it's about, they have to pad it out with a bunch of stupid crap about some guy trying to buy the grandma's general store (General store? What is this, 1910?), a kidnapping, jokes about fruitcake, a lawyer named "I. M. Slime" (wow, this cartoon is *so witty*), "reindeer nip" (like catnip, only stupid), and tons more mind-numbing idiocy that doesn't have anything to do with anything. This is *literally* the worst Xmas special ever, and at one point even Wikipedia agreed. (It's gone now, but a while back some Christmas hero appended "This movie sucks." to its page.) Fuck, fuck, fuck this cartoon and everyone who had anything to do with it. I hope the only thing they get for Christmas is coal in their stockings. Coal or cancer.

The Great Santa Claus Caper
(1978)

This ISO-9000 type (he looks like Wile E. Coyote's long-lost cousin), decides to take over Santa's operation because it isn't efficient. His plan is to encase all the toys in blocks of plastic so you can't actually play with them, then charge *more* for them anyway! Wait a minute, I get it: he's not ISO-9000 - he works for the Comic Book Grading Company! Wow, he really *is* a irredeemable fucking asshole. Fortunately, it turns out that the opposite of the Comic Book Grading Company is love, so Raggedy Ann & Andy are able to save all the toys. Normally I think the messages in Christmas specials are pretty gay, but I totally agree with this one, so if you know a person who collects toys but never takes them out of the packages you should tear those fuckers open and give them to some kids to play with this Christmas. Ultimately that person will thank you, I promise.

The Greatest Adventure: Stories from the Bible
The Nativity
(1987)

When I was a kid my parents always set up this "nativity scene" under the Christmas tree, so one year my cousin and I decided that it was time for G.I. Joe to travel back in time and destroy Christmas. It didn't work out the way they planned though, because Baby Jesus used his telekinetic powers to fuck their worlds and the only one who survived was Lady Jaye (the Three Wise Men rescued her so they could run a train on her hot little Real American Hero ass). I was kind of hoping this cartoon would play out along similar lines, seeing as it *does* involve time travel, but of course it didn't. Instead, it's the same old story: God rolls in, knocks boots with this broad, she shacks up in a barn with her sucker husband, the Wise Guys* roll up with some bling, she pops out the kid, and finally the riff-raff show up to gawk. The only difference this time is that the three time-traveling teens from the other *Greatest Adventure Stories from the Bible* cartoons (a guy, a hot chick, and a vagrant) tag along and engage in pointless antics along the way. Besides the hottie of course, the only good thing about this was the incredibly irritable Roman dude they assigned to follow the Three Wise

Cats and report back. ("Yes, yes, and if they fall on their knees before some squalling baby report right back...you only have to tell me once.")

I'm not sure how any of this qualifies as an "adventure" story. Where the hell is G.I. Joe when you really need them?

---

*For some reason one of them is dressed like a spare wizard from *The Hobbit* in this version.

He-Man/She-Ra: A Christmas Special
(1985)

He-Man toys were cool as hell, but for some reason the clowns who produced the cartoon decided to fuck everything up. For one thing, they made everyone a goddamn retard: the bad guys were all deformed monsters and terrifying demons, but all they ever did was fall down, and nobody could figure out who He-Man really was just because he took off his shirt. Plus it was mind-blowingly homoerotic: He-Man's big move, for example, was to grab a bad guy from behind, in a bear hug, and repeatedly dry-hump his ass. The show was super popular regardless, so they followed up with a version for girls called *She-Ra*. Now She-Ra was pretty fine, and all her friends were smokin' hot mermaids and butterfly chicks and shit, so it was actually *less* gay to be into the girl-themed version. How fucked up is that?

In this special, some Earth kids visit He-Man's planet and immediately start witnessing to everybody. The bad guys (understandably) decide to waste them, so this one of them kidnaps them and flees in an inarguably penis-shaped helicopter. And if you think I'm pulling a Freud and reading way too much into it, the part, moments later, where a giant seizes the helicopter will dispel all doubts. I kid you not, it's even more blatant than the cover of Judas Priest's *Turbo*. If that was the only homoerotic content in this cartoon maybe you could argue it was just a coincidence or something, but almost everyone dresses like they're on their way to a gay pride parade, there's rainbows *everywhere*, and there's even a part where a guy plays the *lute*. You don't have to be a genius to put the pieces together here. The *only* straight thing about this show is about half-way through, where you can freeze-frame an upskirt shot of She-Ra. Too bad she's wearing panties.

Holiday Reunion
(2003)

For some reason National Lampoon, whoever or whatever that is, can't stop making *Vacation* movies, even though the post-1980s installments are so fucking bad that even Clark Griswold won't do them, and he was in *Funny Farm*. In this one, Rosewood from *Beverly Hills Cop* visits his long-lost cousin for Thanksgiving, but then the worst possible thing happens: it turns out that the cousin is a hippie. Of course you know the hippie and his family are going to do all these crazy things and freak Rosewood's family out, but in the end they'll learn to love and accept each other and you'll throw up and wish you never put this piece of fucking crap in your Netflix queue in the first place. There are only two good things about this stupid movie: Rosewood's daughter is hot enough to make your balls finally drop, and the hippie's crazy-ass daughter is even hotter. Naturally I spent the whole movie hoping that at least one of them would get naked, or maybe out of nowhere some lesbian *Flowers in the Attic* kissin' cousins stuff might start going on. Of course that didn't happen (weak), but they *did* engage in a catfight, in the mud, which was fucking **awesome**. (We never see their tits though, because the people who made this movie didn't want to compromise their artistic vision by putting anything entertaining in it.) If there was more of that sort of thing going on this movie might've been at least passable, but mostly it was shit like an old guy farting or Rosewood falling down a hill. There are a *few* things less funny than farting and falling down (crib death, for example), but not very many, so if that's the best you can come up maybe you should find a new line of work, National Lampoon. This subpar shit just isn't cutting it.

Holiday Switch

(2007)

Ah, yes. Every year, just after Thanksgiving, my dad replaced our usual beatin' strap with the "holiday switch", which was painted to look like a candy cane and even had little pieces of tinsel glued to it. He was a real comedian, my dad. I promise you, they will *never* find his body.

So anyway, the main chick in this movie is starting to think that maybe she married the wrong guy. Oh, boo-hoo. Here's a litmus test for you, bitch: if he doesn't cheat with anyone uglier than you or hit you where you can't hide the bruises, count your blessings. Believe me, that's the best you can hope for, because this is a Lifetime movie and on Lifetime they're *all* creeps. Except for the hilarious, flamboyantly gay designer who helped you plan your sister's zany, last-minute wedding. Oh, and the total catch who's married to your best friend, but he's possessed by a ghost.

Seriously though, I've been ~~the cause of~~ privy to plenty of unhappy marriages, and compared to some of them ("Arnold says it's technically a miscarriage, because he didn't *plan* on punching me in the stomach. He was drunk.") this trick's "broke and vaguely dissatisfied" grievances really aren't cutting it. Nevertheless, in a moment so fucking surreal that I still can't believe it happened, a moment that, in fact, may even reflect some accidental depth, she crawls through the dryer into an alternate universe where she married a different cat who's so fucking rich that he hires someone else to shit silver dollars *for* him. She doesn't seem too surprised by any of this, either. I guess she reads a lot of comic books. Of course she ultimately learns that being rich isn't always better (what?), and in the end it turns out it was all a dream. I don't recall if Christmas was also saved in the process, but if it was that would definitely be the trifecta.

Holiday Wishes
(2006)

You know, even if a story is really long and super complicated you should be able to describe it in two sentences or less. *War and Peace* (1424 pages) is about Napoleon invading Russia. *Varney the Vampire* (868 pages) is about a vampire. Named Varney. *Atlas Shrugged* (1168 pages) is about a bunch of pretentious horseshit. This movie though would take a week to explain. We've got an orphan and a rich girl swapping bodies, the lesbo from *Buffy the Vampire Slayer* looking for her long-lost sister, some guy who turns out to be a ghost creeping around... Even if you do manage to sort out this movie's endless, unrelated plots it still doesn't make any sense because in addition to being hopelessly complicated it's also badly put together. Hell, for several minutes I thought the orphan was the missing sister, and that all her parts were like a flashback or something.

It's a fucking disaster, and even ogling the Buffy chick's phat ass doesn't help, as it does with so many other things. ☹

Holidays

(2016)

This horror anthology features stories about several holidays, including St. Patrick's Day, Father's Day, and (of course) Halloween, which if you ask me has been done to death and should have been excised in favor of something more original. Maybe Arbor Day. Anyway, the Christmas episode concerns this dork who wants to get his kid the hot new toy for Christmas, and rather than allowing his quest to deteriorate into *Jingle All the Way* levels of slapstick jackassery opts to steal one from a dying man instead. The toy, it turns out, is some sort of virtual reality gizmo that's infused with the memories of the dead guy, so in the end it's just an halfassed update of any given horror movie where someone gets an organ transplant and starts experiencing the organ donor's memories, but with a dumb, *Lawnmower Man* twist. It's pretty forgettable, and the other stories aren't much better. The standout, St. Patrick's Day, is funny and repulsive and absurd and should've been a whole movie, but the rest of them are either obvious, stupid, boring, or a painful combination of the three. Just one more reason to hate the holidays. All of them.

How the Grinch Stole Christmas!
(1992)

I've watched so many awful Christmas abortions it's fucking unreal, and I don't mean the kind your sister got last year. So now I'm gonna settle down with a *good* Xmas special: *The Grinch*. Yeah, I know the Grinch sells out in the end, but there's so much cool shit in this cartoon up to that point: the animal abuse, the stealing, the being narrated by none other than goddamned Frankenstein's Monster himself...

WHAT THE BABY JESUS-PUNTING HELL???????

What the piss is this? Where's that video box? "Narrated by Walter Matthau"? The Bad News Bears' *coach*? What the fuck? This isn't the Grinch! It's barely a cartoon at all! They blink once in a while, but that's about it. There are seriously no quantifiers in the English language to explain how lame this is, and if it wasn't for Jim Carrey it would be the worst version of the Grinch of all time. What a ripoff. What an ass-reaming. What a complete and utter hose job. This *should* be called "How Random House Home Video Stole My Eight Bucks". Cocksucking shit parasites. Fuck these pricks.

Note: Also includes *If I Ran the Zoo*. Fuck that one, too.

How to Marry a Billionaire - A Christmas Tale
(2000)

These three cats are fed up with being broke and dating money-grubbing whores. Frankly I'm kind of impressed that they somehow managed to do both. At any rate, they decide they need to meet some rich broads, and a romantic comedy ensues. I don't know how a movie like this ended up being kind of good, but they actually achieved this, which I'd say counts as a bona fide Xmas miracle. There is one lazy jumping to conclusions/misunderstanding bit near the end, and the wrap-up is entirely too convenient, but by then we've gotten several legitimately funny jokes, a chick complaining that she's 25 and "doesn't have a lot of time left" to which one guy replies "You've been watching the WB again, haven't you?", and a part where one of the secondary guys finally succeeds in his chosen profession after years of failure solely because he was on drugs. The actual Christmas connection, frankly, is barely even. There's not a flake of snow to be seen, no reindeer, not even any Christmas magic. And while Christmas magic is, at best, my fourth favorite kind of magic (behind stage magic, black magic, and bunny magic) you still kind of expect at least a little bit of it in a goddamned Xmas movie. Fuck it, though; this one actually didn't suck, so I'm not gonna look a gift horse in the dick.

I Saw Mommy KISSING Santa Claus

(2001)

I have no idea why "kissing" is in all caps. Maybe we're meant to understand it as a euphemism for "fucking". Or maybe it's a really intense kiss, like the kind where one person is using their tongue and the other one is using their penis. Around here, we call that a "job interview".

At any rate, in this movie a kid catches mom and dad engaging in a some G-rated Xmas role playing, with dad as Santa and mom as the naughty little girl. He's too young to go on a brutal killing spree though [cf. *Santa Claws*, later in this book], so he decides to do the next best thing and act like an out-of-control little bastard. He's strictly amateur hour at first, but before long he graduates to petty theft and simple assault, so I'll begrudgingly give him some props. And putting Jarts in the fireplace in an attempt to impale Santa when he comes down the chimney was a pretty clever idea, although I have to question where this kid got his hands on Jarts seeing as they've been banned in the U.S. since 1988. (Coincidentally, this is the same year the U.S. banned not being a fucking pussy.)

Of course an endless parade of idiot coincidences and misunderstandings ensues to keeps this idiot plot rolling (because that's so much easier for the writer than making any effort whatsoever) until the moronic ending, where the kid nearly kills his dad with a bunch of *Home Alone* style slapstick traps intended for Santa. (Oh, and don't think for a second that this kid is doing any this shit reluctantly or whatever. He's laughing his ass off the whole time and clearly enjoying it. He even smiles at the end when he realizes that he's seriously injured an innocent old man. He's a legitimate sociopath.)

Of course the whole misunderstanding is cleared up eventually (i.e. when approximately 90-100 minutes has passed and it's time to wrap things up), but instead of doling out the crippling, life-altering beating out main kid so richly deserves, everyone rewards the little bastard for his antisocial behavior, even the *real* Santa Claus! It's unbelievable. And does this movie really need *five fucking endings?* Seriously, it just won't fucking stop. Go away, *I Saw Mommy KISSING Santa Claus*. Nobody wants you here.

I'll Be Home for Christmas

(1998)

Remember when the kid from *Home Improvement* became a "teen heartthrob" for a while? Dark days, right? Well in this flick his dad offers to give him a 1957 Porsche if he comes home for Christmas, which pretty much ensures that the three people watching this who don't already hate his fucking guts will now. Due to a wacky felony though he ends up having to hitchhike home, while dressed as Santa Claus, and madcap misadventures ensue. Needless to say this movie sucks the shit right out of a reindeer's ass. I did like the parts where the *Home Improvement* kid got hurt, but he was never injured seriously enough for these to be entirely satisfying. And, okay, it is pretty hot when his girlfriend sings "Doctor Jones". Too bad she grew up to be Jessica Biel.

Inspector Gadget Saves Christmas

(1992)

This cartoon opens at Santa's sweatshop, I mean workshop, where all the elves are waking up to make toys. Every single one of these elves looks exactly the same, except for *one* who appears to be in charge, and there aren't any *girl* elves, so I'm guessing they're all imperfect clones of that one, which is an interesting insight into how Santa runs his sick operation. Things get even worse though when a supervillain shows up, possesses the elves, throws Santa in the dungeon,* and takes the whole dump over. As my six-year-old nephew always says when his dad breaks out the whiskey, "It looks like Christmas is fucked!"

Not quite, though, because Inspector Gadget is on the case. Inspector Gadget is basically *Get Smart!* crossed with Machine Man, so the big joke is that he can't do anything right. Needless to say that joke gets old fast, but if you're into *Get Smart!* you're probably used to that by now. *Get Smart!* only had three jokes and was on for what, fifty years? If you're into Machine Man, on the other hand, I don't know what to tell you. Maybe you should get out of the house more.

---

*You kind of have to wonder why Santa Claus has a dungeon in the first place. Just what the fuck is going on up there?

Jingle All the Way
(1996)

The only black guy less funny than Sinbad is the one who's dating your daughter, and the only thing funny about Arnold Schwarzenegger is the fact that he exists, and yet somehow, through some evil Christmas magic, this movie is totally hilarious. It's got Sinbad getting so worked up over toy commercials that he chokes a bitch; a riot while ironic Xmas music plays; a pedophile joke; a midget punched in the face so hard that he flies across the room; a donnybrook involving dozens of police, Santas, and elves; the flaming head of one of the Three Wise Dudes kicked through a window at some carolers; Arnold punching out a reindeer; and tons of violence and property destruction. Why so many people hate this flick is beyond me; hell, even that fatass movie critic Siskel N. Ebert said it was okay, and he hates almost everything that doesn't have mayonnaise on it. For real, what a bunch of humorless fucks.

Joe Santa Claus

(1951)

Joe Santa Claus? *Joe momma!* Ha ha ha! So anyway, the front office informs this salesman that he's the most expendable employee in the store, so he has to play Santa Claus this year. This totally sets him off, and he spends the next several minutes whining about his kraut ex-wife, who he met while he was stationed in Germany after the war. (Apparently someone wasn't paying attention during *Your Job in Germany*.) He blathers on and on about the good times (teaching her the names of vegetables, smoking), and the bad (fights about his rampant sexism and overall laziness), but apparently the main reason they broke up was because he couldn't hold a job. So what's the first thing he does when she says she'll give him another chance? He takes an unannounced leave of absence from work! Good call, Mr. Most Expendable. Your can clean out your locker after the holiday.

And thus began the endless cycle of poverty, blame, and domestic violence that lead inevitably to the death of Mrs. Joe Santa Claus in 1954. Mr. Joe was sent to the gas chamber in 1956. Their daughter ran away after being placed in a home by the state and was never seen again. Merry Christmas!

Karroll's Christmas
(2004)

I swear, if I see one more version of *A Christmas Carol* this year, I'll fucking puke. Actually, I'll probably puke either way, because I drink too much. At least this one promises to get it backwards, and it delivers, sort of. See, this time around the ghosts have the wrong address, so they end up hassling a completely innocent guy with their tired old shtick. It sounds like a one-note gag, but they do manage to wring a few decent bits out of it, including a totally unexpected gay joke that actually made me laugh out loud. I also liked the part where one of the ghosts explains that there's no sitting in Hell ("It doesn't sound like much, does it? But after a couple of years...") and the fact that Death is a midget. They even give the only truly awesome version of the original (the one with George C. Scott) props by showing a few seconds of it on TV. It all falls apart during the home stretch though. The main guy decides to help out the cat the ghosts were *supposed* to visit (it's that joker who had dinner with Andre) and from here the whole thing deteriorates into the usual puddle of steaming, sappy crap.

But let's end this one on a positive note, because I'm generally a positive person: the main guy's girlfriend in this movie is so staggeringly fine that every time she smiles a thousand angels go to Hell for experiencing their first orgasm, and she's cool as fuck to boot. By way of example, on Xmas Eve she walks in wearing most of a sexy Santa outfit and a tag that says "To Allen: One pair of ankles. Do not open until Christmas". My god, that is just beyond incredible. If I had a girlfriend like that, I'd fuck her.

The Legend of the Candy Cane

(2001)

I know exactly what you're thinking: "There's a legend of the candy cane?" Well, according to this cartoon the red stripes are actually the "sadness of Jesus" or some crazy bullshit. Okay, I never heard *that* one before so I looked it up and sure enough: it's pussified here, but Christians really do think that the red in a candy cane is *Jesus blood*. Ugh - I'll never eat a candy cane again. That disgusting story only takes a couple of minutes to tell though, so the rest of the running length is padded out with some *Little House on the Prairie* types rescuing this girl from a hole (coincidentally, this was the plot of the vast majority of *Little House on the Prairie* episodes), and a horse, a mountain goat, a dog, and an owl (natural allies in the wild) engaging in antics, being chased by a wolf, and helping the goat get over his fear of heights. There is a surprising amount of climactic synergy when the end features the goat overcoming his fear of heights and jumping into the hole to save the chick from the wolf (the only way they could've tied it all together any more neatly is if someone pulled her out of the hole with a giant candy cane afterwards), but that doesn't make this any less awful. And really, Christians, why does everything always have to be soaked in blood before you'll put it in your mouth? What the hell is wrong with you people?

The Leprechauns' Christmas Gold
(1981)

This kid rows to an uncharted island to get a Christmas tree, but he ends up freeing an evil fairy who has it in for the local mickrechauns. (Ha! "**Mick**rechauns". Get it?) See, she needs their gold by Christmas morning or she'll die, but she's not allowed to steal it and they won't give it to her. One of the potato-sucking little bastards gives the kid the gold for safe keeping, but he turns out to be incomprehensibly stupid; all the fairy has to do is disguise herself as a cute chick and he just hands it right over. Ah, the power of pussy. But then, in a move made famous by Dracula, she putzes around until the sun comes up and dies anyway. Are you kidding me? For real, she had *all fucking night* to go get the damn gold! What the hell was she off doing that could possibly be more important? Scrolling TikTok? Taking a nap? Jesus.

They made a shitload of these damn puppet-toon Xmas shows back in the day and a few of them have become Christmas classics or at least staples, but I think they were really scraping the bottom of the barrel when they came up with this one. I mean seriously, Christmas leprechauns? What the fuck?

The Little Brown Burro and The Christmas Raccoons
(1978/1980)

This VHS tape has two cartoons on it - I never heard of the first one, but they used to show the Raccoon one on Canadian TV all the time, which should tell you plenty right there. *The Little Brown Burro* is about a donkey who keeps complaining because he's too small to work. What a moron. Anyway, this rat becomes his friend and they wander around and sing some shitty songs and finally he gets to be the donkey that carries Jesus's mom around right before she pops out the kid, like that's anything to brag about. Yeah, I was the guy who sold Lee Harvey Oswald the bullets, too. Big deal. In the second cartoon, some raccoons end up homeless because this evil pink aardvark who runs a lumber company cuts down their house and then these kids steal it and use it for their Christmas tree. It's just like that one old cartoon where those two gay squirrels lose their tree, except that one was actually sort of funny. Obviously some clown picked up the rights to two lame Christmas cartoons over a game of poker or something, and they figured they'd clean up if they put them both out on one videotape. They really didn't think it through though, because one of the cartoons is religious and the other one is a bunch of tree-hugging hippie crap, so inevitably most people will hate one or the other. Actually, most people will probably hate both of them, because they suck.

Meet the Santas

(2005)

This is actually *Single Santa Seeks Mrs. Claus Part 2*, so the chances of it being good are slim and none and Crystal Bernard getting naked just left town. In Part 1 Santa Jr. had to find a wife before Christmas, but of course he waited until the very last minute and a crappy movie ensued. This time around they have to be *officially* married before... I dunno, some... *other*... Christmas. It doesn't actually make a whole lot of sense if you stop and think about it, so I won't. Anyway, they wait until the last minute again and this opens up a whole can of shit because 1) you can never tell a chick she only has like a week to plan her wedding and 2) if they aren't actually legal by Christmas, Christmas will explode. Or something. It's all pretty dumb; I just spent the whole movie whacking it to Crystal Bernard.

Mother Krampus

(2017)

This flick is about *Frau Perchta*, an obscure Christmas bogey/witch who supposedly gutted bad children alive and then stuffed them full of rocks. Good children got a piece of silver for looking the other way and keeping their mouths shut. Pretty tasty stuff, but Krampus was the big holiday horror fad circa Christmas 2017 so the movie ended up saddled with a Krampus-adjacent title instead. I guess we're just lucky that they didn't call it "Mother Elf on the Shelf". Anyway, our witch's primary focus this year is a little fat girl and her family and assorted acquaintances. The witch in question would probably be a lot scarier if they didn't portray her as, essentially, a homeless person, what with her little camp in the woods and her propensity for hoarding cats, and the movie quickly wears out its welcome with too many "shocking" (read: dumb) (not to mention predictable) revelations and ridiculous bits. (The part where the dad "comes around" and promises the mom that he'll fix their marriage rings so false that I laughed my ass off, same as I did when my own dad tried to sell my mom a similar bill of goods.) That said, it is gory, and there are several superior brunette hotties on hand. Wherever this was filmed, the people making babies do nice work. There's no tits though, and what's Christmas without tits? It's AKA **X**mas for a reason, you know. If you want to see a little fat girl menaced by a witch, there are any number of variations on "Hansel and Gretel" out there, and I'll bet there's even a porn version if you're really hung up on the tits thing. *Mother Krampus* is eminently skippable.

Mr. St. Nick

(2002)

It's time for Santa Claus to retire and Frasier is supposed to take his place, so Santa starts losing his powers* and Frasier starts gaining them. Frasier's already got his hands full though: some con artists are looting his Christmas charity, plus Immigration wants to bust his cook. I suppose if you're an illegal wetback Immigration *might* be out to ruin your Christmas, but unless the plot is about that specific situation they're a pretty dumb choice for the bad guy in a Christmas movie. And the part where Santa thinks that someone dressing as him in a TV commercial for a charity is an insult to the Claus family name is pretty retarded. If *that* bothers him, I wonder how he feels about *The Tits That Saved XXX-mas* (2003)?

Anyway, things really go south when Immigration finds out about the missing money and Frasier takes the fall. Uh, since when does Immigration investigate fraud? Frasier's even interrogated by an Immigration agent! This movie must've been written by a Mexican and the only bad guys he could think of were INS and the Chupacabras, so he just picked the least ridiculous one. Actually, he probably should've gone with the Chupacapras. That movie would've been a lot more interesting than this one is.

All his powers. "I can't get it up!" he says in one part.

Ms. Scrooge

(1997)

The people who make movies never get tired of trotting this Scrooge shit out, do they? Lazy fucks. For real, how many different versions of this fucking movie do we need? I say five, tops: an old black & white one; a fairly new one; one for black people so *they* don't piss and moan; a reverse version where a nice guy gets fed up with Christmas and learns to hate it; and a porno version. That's plenty. Think about it, if they made three or four new versions of *Independence Day* every year – all featuring the exact same story – people wouldn't stand for it (hell, I punched an old lady in the face over the first one), so why do we put up with this crap?

I guess this could count as the black one since Scrooge is black this time around (he's a woman too, but that actually works because I can totally see black people naming their daughter "Ebenita"). Of course it sucks, but that's no surprise since black people almost always get the short end of the movie stick (example: *Big Momma's House*). At any rate, it's the same old story: "Ebenita" Scrooge is all greedy and selfish, so on Christmas Eve a bunch of ghosts show up and give her the holiday business. Oh, and did I mention that all of these ghosts are white people? White ghosts, huh? They might as well have just had the KKK roll on up in there and set her straight. Why is it folks are all "woke" 99% of the time and you can't even stand outside the Immigration office eating Taco Bell without somebody blowing their stack, but then they never call people out on blatant, obvious shit like this? It's absolutely bewildering.

Naughty or Nice
(2004)

I know sports are for people who aren't quite smart enough to understand regular television, with all its confusing *CSI* spin-offs and complicated sitcoms starring percentages of men, but even that doesn't explain sports radio. Seriously, where do they find the cretinous sub-fucks who support that shit? This flick is already operating on a pretty faulty assumption – that people think George Lopez is funny – so you can imagine how awful it gets when you throw some sports radio stuff *and* Christmas into the mix. The story: George Lopez is a sports radio guy who finds out that being nice makes the local sports teams win, so he changes the format of his dickish show and learns the true magic of enjoying sports on Christmas. I never thought I'd see a sports movie with a dumber premise than *Field of Dreams* (guy builds a baseball field that raises the dead, so they can play baseball), and I still haven't, but this is a pretty close second. Anyway, it turns out that the people who listen to talk radio prefer ignorant shitbags (as if the continued success of Michael Savage, Alex Jones, Paul Molloy, and about a million others didn't make that abundantly clear), so his ratings drop like a rock and his selfish cunt wife (who thinks that being the victim of assault & battery and ending up in the hospital is no excuse for missing a Christmas recital) leaves him.

It looks like he's completely boned, but suddenly everyone decides that they like his new approach after all, and it must be an Xmas miracle because they never do explain how or why this happens. Of course, his lame-ass television program did run for six seasons (six!), so I guess when George Lopez puts his mind to it, anything is possible.

New Year's Evil
(1980)

Of all the old-school holiday slasher movies, this one definitely has the weakest gimmick. So this guy kills one person when midnight strikes in each time zone, so what? There's only four time zones in the United States, so even if he has to kill a couple of pesky witnesses along the way we're looking at a grand total six murders, tops. Jason Voorhees wouldn't even get out of bed if there were only six people to murder. This guy is no Jason Voorhees though. In fact, he might be the most hilariously hapless slasher ever. His first kill, at least, goes off without a hitch, although he fucks her first and she's pretty ugly. The second one is this twit he picks up at a bar, and she's so ditzy and annoying that he nearly goes batshit waiting for midnight to roll around so he can finally off her. Number three (who's pretty fucking cute, I must say) actually manages to escape when the cops show up just in time, and frankly I'm surprised our boy is even able to go on after this because movie serial killers tend to be pretty OCD about their meticulous little gimmicks and generally lose it when something like this happens. Maybe he let it slide because the whole thing was building up to victim #4 anyway, the one he *really* wants to kill, but by then the police have determined his identity and they prevent him from icing her, too. So, ultimately, this loser barely scored a 50%, and that isn't even taking into account the part where he accidentally rear-ends some bikers and they chase him down and nearly beat the shit out of him. On the plus side, the plot does manage one good twist, the cute chick who gets away (just barely) shows some nip, and there's a hilariously fake head. It's hard to get behind a slasher this goddamned incompetent though, and even putting that aside entirely too much of this movie is padded out with supposed punkers* dancing to laughably fake punk bands. (Although I did kinda like the song "Dumb Blondes".) You know how, no matter how carefully you plan, and how shitfaced you get, New Year's Eve always turns out sort of lame? Well the same thing holds true for *New Year's Evil*.

***Punker** (n) One who punks

The Night Before Christmas

(2004)

Are you familiar with the "uncanny valley"? That's what you call it when something looks enough like a real person – but still off in some indefinable way – that it subconsciously freaks you out. It's why the movie *Shrek* makes your girlfriend wake up screaming. Well, that's what the people in this cartoon are like, and the animals aren't much better. Oh, and the story sucks, too. Basically, one of Santa's ~~elves~~ fairies decides to be Lucifer to his Yahweh, so this mouse who overheard his evil plan tracks down the Fairy Queen (who, for some reason, doesn't have legs) and she puts a stop to it. Not that the evil fairy was anything but hopeless anyway; how seriously can you take someone who sounds like Butters from *South Park*? Bonuses include a sing-along (as if anyone would ever want to hear the awful, awful songs from this cartoon again), a docu-bit about the broad who created this ("Today her art is loved by just about everyone who speaks English!" Ego the Living Planet has nothing on this bitch.), and a shitload of ads before the main feature that you can't skip no matter what you do. If you don't already hate Christmas, watching everything on this DVD will probably do the trick.

The Night Before the Night Before Christmas

(2010)

You mean St. Victoria Day? Things have proper names you know, and you should really consider learning some of them so you stop sounding like a goddamned retard. Just the other day I heard this lady asking a sales clerk if they had any "seasons on regular". Any non-moron would assume she was trying to order food (or suffering a stroke), but after several minutes of confusion it turned out she was looking for *television shows on DVD*. Jesus fucking Christ, only in Pinellas Park.

Anyway, this movie really expects us to buy that Santa Claus somehow got his wires crossed and starts delivering presents on December 23rd. I'm sorry, but I refuse to believe that Santa would run such a slipshod operation. Okay, maybe the *Home Improvement* Santa from the *Santa Clause* movies, because he's a goddamned drunk, but otherwise, no way. As it turns out though, this Santa's staggering incompetence doesn't end there. In short order he falls off a roof, suffers amnesia, loses his bag of toys, and misplaces his own dick (probably). Now it's up to this typical all-American family (i.e. middle class and white) to jog his memory and save Christmas by, naturally, being extra, extra Christmasy. There's just one (more) problem: this family is *totally dysfunctional*. The parents work a lot and even when they're home they're on the phone with work a lot and... uh, really that's pretty much it. *That's* what this movie considers dysfunctional??? I recall a childhood family Thanksgiving where my dad *literally* threw a frozen turkey through a plate glass window (he was aiming for my stepsister). Movie, you don't fucking *know* dysfunctional. Speaking of teenage girls I would totally make out with whether it was appropriate or not, the teenage daughter in this movie is pretty hot and gets all the best lines, and it's a shame Santa fixes her "dysfunctional" family in the end because in my experience chicks from dysfunctional families are way more likely to put out on the first date. Or even within a hour of meeting them, sometimes.

The Night They Saved Christmas
(1984)

I never understand these scenes in movies where people are engaged in some complicated activity but have to wrap it up because it's time for the kids to go to school. Are there really entire families who roll out of bed at 4 AM on a weekday so they can get some snowmobiling in before breakfast? Then again, this movie does take place near the arctic circle, so maybe they're smack dab in the middle of 47 days of sunlight and decided to just stay up straight through. Sleep deprivation would certainly help explain the complex, detailed hallucinations in which they visit "North Pole City" and meet Santa Claus. Not to mention everyone's inexplicable obsession with an evil, behind-the-scenes mastermind they call "Gaylord". For real, this Gaylord character is accused of everything from kidnapping to dosing people with hallucinogens to trying to trick an oil company into drilling in the wrong place, but we never once see the guy and as far as I can tell he doesn't actually exist. Hell, by the end just about everyone in this movie meets or at least sees Santa Claus, but we never *once* lay eyes on this Gaylord joker. As for Santa, I did dig his setup, what with the Star Trek transporter mounted to his sleigh and the cool-ass reindeer that look like something out of an old-school Sinbad movie, but man, I just couldn't get past the remainder of these crackpots and their paranoid Gaylord delusion. There is no fucking Gaylord, dammit!

A Norman Rockwell Christmas

(1993)

I know Norman Rockwell was that one corny painter, but I never entirely understood what folks meant by "A Norman Rockwell Christmas". I always assumed it was code for "No black people". This documentary starts out telling us about the actual guy, but mostly they just show his paintings while generic Xmas music plays. They also trot out some kid actor nobody ever heard of to make stupid comments, but fortunately we don't see *too* much of him and after a while he just sits there looking as bored as we are. It's the type of time-filler crap they always show on television on Christmas Eve and thenabouts because most people are busy doing Christmas stuff or at least getting drunk and no one's watching anyway. It sucks because frankly I kinda wanted to get the dirt on this guy; seriously, wouldn't it be awesome to find out that he beat his wife or passed out Nazi literature during his spare time or something? Oh well, at least his granddaughter shows up, and she's pretty fine. I'd sure like to ring the bells on *her* hot little Bobtail. Too bad gramps never did a painting of her in the nude. At least that we know of.

North Pole Nutrias

(2002)

These two nutria puppets (for those of you unfamiliar, nutrias are basically swimming rats, except there are some people who actually like rats) are summoned to the North Pole to combat an evil virus that's melting all the toys. When they get there (by rocket ship) they attend a meeting with several other animal puppets, but before the puppets can hash out a plan the virus shows up, plays a rock song, and melts the only toys left. Nobody can figure out what to do so they all take a break and go to some shows on the North Pole strip. Santa Claus himself introduces these shows, and while he has the body of a puppet, he has a real person's head, played by a weird-looking old dude who sounds like he's half in the bag. The first show is just some fat hippie in a red suit and a nasty-ass broad who looks like Tammy Faye Bakker singing a Christmas song. It's pretty lame, but the next one more than makes up for it: it's this guy playing a weird techno song on a fucked-up synthesizer, backed by a reindeer puppet on drums and this amazingly hot chick on maracas. I'd sure like to find her under the tree on Xmas morning. Anyway, everyone agrees that this dude's synthesizer is so cool that every kid would want one for Christmas, so the elves manufacture a run of them to replace all the melted toys. The virus shows up again to ruin everything and starts bashing the girl nutria's head in, but then the other nutria shoves a pie down its throat, it dies, and Christmas is saved. I presume this is trying (a bit too hard, in my opinion) to be the most fucked-up holiday special ever, but it just doesn't hold a candle to truly deranged and misguided shit like *A Family Circus Christmas*. Then again, the Family Circus didn't have a killer hottie playing maracas.

The Nuttiest Nutcracker

(1999)

Gaaaah! The last, the very last, thing I want to encounter during the holidays, or ever, are creepy, uncanny valley, *Polar Express*-style cartoon people. Seriously, who comes up with these cartoons or thinks for even one second that they're actually a good idea? Just because you *can* do something with a computer doesn't always mean you should.

So, everybody knows the story of the Nutcracker. Except me, come to think of it. I'm pretty sure it doesn't involve actual talking nuts though, so I guess that's this version's gimmick. The nuts come to life to help this girl after she wishes that Christmas would disappear forever, just because her parents are going to be a little late getting home on Christmas Eve. Talk about a fucking drama queen. So what do the nuts do? They use Christmas magic to shrink the self-absorbed bitch down to their size and then smash her fucking face in. Oh, sorry, that was just wishful hoping on my part. Actually, and I'm not kidding this time, they all go to sleep! Brilliant. It's a good thing the bad guy in this story is a bit more proactive: he's the Mouse King, and he wants to kidnap the nuts and put them to work in his cheese mines (because those exist). As an added bonus, somehow this will destroy

Christmas. I'd go on, but there's really no point since this whole plot is just random, incomprehensible gibberish from start to finish, although I would be lax in not mentioning the part where the Mouse King decides that he wants to *fuck the human girl,* even though she's like a thousand times his size. There's only two possible ways for that kind of forbidden love to play out, and they both usually end with a particularly humiliating visit to the emergency room.

Incidentally, the titular (heh) Nutcracker in this cartoon is way too small to actually put nuts into and therefore, technically, isn't even a nutcracker at all. Way to entirely miss the point, assholes.

One Hell of a Christmas

(2002)

This crook swipes some supernatural thingamabob, and when he leaves it at his buddy's house everything goes all *Evil Dead 2* on the guy: a dead hooker attacks him with kung fu, a stuffed toy tries to claw his face off, and a cowboy from a wall poster comes to life and tries to shoot him. Then, just when you think it's all over, he gets sucked down his toilet into Hell. Obviously this is a flick with a lot of good ideas, but they manage to screw it the vast majority of it. For one thing, the main guy is Mexican so they *should've* called it "Feliz Navi-Dead". That would've been hilarious. It's bad enough that they didn't think of that, but there's not enough gore, either, and worst of all they outfit a redheaded hooker in bondage gear and a Santa Claus hat but somehow forget to show her naked. In the end the Devil turns up to get the thingamabob back because it turns out it's his *coke nail* (I'm not fucking kidding), which is just fucked-up enough (especially for a Christmas movie) to save this from completely sucking ass, but next time *show the hooker naked*, idiots.

The Phantom of the Open Hearth
(1976)

Everyone was up in arms and shitting crumb cake when they (inevitably) went and made *A Christmas Story 2*, somehow forgetting that their precious Part 1 was a goddamned remake in the first place. Well, not *exactly*, but this movie does feature (a different) Ralphie, (a different) The Old Man, the same annoying narrator guy, and even the saga of the infamous leg lamp. Ralphie's in high school in this version though, so he's less concerned with BB guns and more concerned with this piece named Daphne Bigelow who, the voice in his head informs us, "offers ecstasies not yet plumbed by human experience". That means he's pretty sure she's a virgin. And rest assured, lovable Ralphie from *A Christmas Story* wants to be the one who pops *that* particular cherry.

Once you disregard the previously noted *Christmas Story* touchstones, the rest of this movie is all over the place though, and it's a tad darker and a lot more low-brow than the take we're all (entirely too) familiar with. For example, there's a surprising amount of drunken puking. My absolute favorite bit is when Ralphie rents a tux for the junior prom and the only jacket in his size has a bullet hole right through the heart and dried blood all over it! I swear to fuck

I'm not making that up. And I was *completely* blindsided by the ending, where the titular Phantom of the Open Hearth goes on a supernatural rampage, killing two of Ralphie's idiot friends and briefly possessing his mom. Okay, fine, I am making that part up.

There's one final, almost meta, element to this movie that I haven't mentioned yet. It begins and ends with Ralphie as an adult, speaking directly to us and waxing incoherent about bumper stickers and his time in the army as he segues into and out of the main story. It's almost like they're intentionally pegging him as exactly the type of annoying bore who tortures family and friends alike with his rambling, pointless stories that have no clear beginning or end and you've all heard at least a dozen times before. Needless to say, this couldn't be more appropriate.

A Pink Christmas
(1978)

I'd love to know what a psychiatrist would say about the Pink Panther. At the beginning of this cartoon he's so destitute that he's fighting stray dogs for food, but when he sees someone unknowingly drop one of their Christmas presents he's scrupulously honest and tries to return it. Yet later, when he actually *does* have a job, he gets this crazy look in his eyes and blatantly steals from a child right in front of everyone. Is he intentionally sabotaging his own success because he possesses cripplingly low self esteem? Or was he overcompensating while poor by behaving in an especially moral fashion, playing to an internalized belief that the universe might subsequently reward him in some manner? Maybe he has Multiple Personality Disorder.

Whatever the case, the Pink Panther is fired. But he refuses to leave the premises without lashing out and destroying some of his former employer's property, so naturally a chase ensues. His low self-esteem now at the forefront of his mental paradigm, the Panther attempts to hide by disguising himself as discount merchandise ("½ off", to be precise). Amazingly, this absurd ploy actually facilitates his escape. Back on the streets, he inexplicably reverts to his antisocial paradigm, again stealing from a child. Once again he's pursued, and this time he's even confronted by law enforcement, but the evidence is destroyed and he ironically manages to avoid the punishment he likely craves.

At this point, unable to reconcile his conflicting psychological needs, the Panther suffers a complete, but mercifully brief, break with reality wherein he's convinced that he has physically transformed into, of all things, a common pigeon.

After a third attempt to steal and a second bid to earn money through gainful employment both fail as a result of his (willful?) incompetence, continued misfortune eventually triggers the re-emergence of the Panther's pseudo-moralistic "bargaining" persona. Once again, he refrains from stealing when given the opportunity, and he even shares a precious, hard-won morsel of food with a stray dog. Eventually his own fractured psyche grants the "reward" for this "selfless" behavior that the external world will not provide: he suffers a complex hallucination wherein a higher power (identified by him, due to his atheistic mindset, as Santa Claus) *does* reward him by providing him with not only a feast, but a Christmas tree as well, both of which he perceives as magically materializing before his very eyes. And so the cycle continues.

Seriously, shrinks, what are you waiting for? This is the kind of case that makes careers.

Pinocchio's Christmas
(1980)

"Pinocchio" my ass. This little fucker looks, and sounds, like Peppermint Patty, and as far as I'm concerned that's who he is. She is. Whatever. So anyway, Peppermint Patty just wants to buy some Christmas presents, but these scheming gypsies bamboozle her out of her money (fucking gypsies; the Nazis had the right idea on that count, at least) so she has no choice but to pursue a career in the theater. She decides to rob her boss the very first night though, and when the reckoning comes due she barely makes it out of town ahead of the law. Later she meets a fairy, gets kidnapped, saves a family's Christmas, hitches a ride with Santa, and (big surprise) takes a lesbian lover.

Definitely weird, and dumb, but it's not all bad: the look on Geppeto's face when they're about to be eaten by the whale is hilarious, and I liked the part where Peppermint Pinocchio decides that Jiminy Cricket is too didactic and tries to smash him with a book. That bit actually comes from the original story, wherein Pinocchio really does kill Jiminy Cricket by smashing him with a hammer. The original also ends with Pinocchio dying a horrible death at the end of a noose as punishment for all his bastard behavior, but, as usual, expecting awesomeness of that caliber from this version was way too much to hope for.

Red Christmas

(2016)

Okay, I realize that this movie takes place in Australia, the land of the rising sun, where our summer is their winter and our up is their down and so on and so forth, but I just can't get behind a Christmas movie – even a horror one – where there's no snow on the ground and everything's all green and southern California-looking. I'm sorry, but this kills the whole Xmas vibe immediately. Are you reading between the lines here, moviemakers who film your Christmas movies in Los Angeles? Because you should really be reading between the lines here.

The setup will be familiar to anyone unfortunate enough to have a family - a parade of unlikable fucks has gathered for the holidays (the Shakespeare-quoting retard is especially annoying) when a coughing, hacking, ominous weirdo shows up at the front door, dressed like he just shuffled off the set of a Blind Dead movie, and starts rambling semi-incoherently about bizarre-ass religious shit and family secrets better left unspoken. In my family this would be my brother, and in addition he'd be late and would've forgotten to bring ice like he promised. The family in this movie doesn't even know the guy though, but they invite him inside anyway (why not?) which turns out to be a mistake because he's a homicidal (literal) failed abortion with a huge chip on his shoulder and you know how *those* people are. (Again, I'm reminded of my brother.) So it's essentially a slasher movie, and, traditionally, the victims in slasher movies tend to be morons, but these characters take the conceit to utterly ludicrous levels. Seriously, how can there be suspense in a movie when everyone is so fucking stupid that they'll clearly do anything – drink poison, stick a fork in a light socket, squander multiple opportunities to simply shoot the killer and wrap this whole thing up with plenty of time left over for Christmas caroling and pie – and are obviously going to die no matter what happens? The only thing I liked about this movie was the sole hottie's T-shirt, which reads "Now I have a fabric pen. Ho ho ho." Other than that it's consistently dumb and tries WAY too hard, like a girl who texts you sixty times the day after a one night stand and tells her friends and family that you're engaged now.

An embarrassment all around.

Richie Rich's Christmas Wish
(1998)

Richie Rich, the richest little prick in the world, wishes he was never born, and thanks to a wishing machine (which of course he only uses for selfish purposes) his wish comes true. So does the little asshole actually disappear forever? We should be so fucking lucky. Instead, the whole world changes around him and now his evil(er) cousin is in charge. So what does Richie do? He goes on a crime spree. I'm dead fucking serious: breaking & entering, dognapping, assault, kidnapping, trespassing, burglary, vandalism, grand theft auto... The list goes on and on. Eventually he ropes a bunch of innocent people into his criminal schemes and they all end up in jail, but in the end he manages to make another wish that puts everything back to normal and everybody has a merry Christmas, except of course the servants who don't even get the day off to spend with their families.

It just goes to show that, in any reality, Richie Rich is a complete piece of shit.

Saint

(2010)

Huh. Apparently the Dutch version of Santa Claus is a major dick. In addition to being the ghost of a complete and utter extortionist bastard, and so politically incorrect that he makes his elves wear blackface, when the full moon falls on December 5th he takes this as the universe giving him the okay to go around killing everybody. And we're not just talking the bad kids, here; naughty or nice, young or old, if Dutch Santa Claus shows up, you better shoot first and ask questions later. (And when you do get around to asking the questions, you should probably do it in Dutch: "Oh, shit, is dat je, Oom Hendrik?")

So, after the setup we meet our three main chicks, who have a walking-home-from-school conversation/scene that's almost exactly like the one in the original *Halloween*. I hope this means we'll get to see one of them stuck in a window later wearing nothing but a shirt and panties. Not long thereafter Dutch Santa arrives, in his Blind Dead-style ghost galleon, utterly demolishing this police boat that's patrolling the river. In short order his posse kills in the vicinity of a dozen people (onscreen) until this crazy cop who knows the score shows the main kid how to settle his holiday hash until the next December 5th full moon or the sequel, whichever comes first. There's lots of action and gore; a cute nurse; a horse crashing through a skylight, sliding out a window, and landing on a police car; someone attacking Santa with a flamethrower; a boat crash; a cop/elf shootout; the ghost galleon blown to pieces; and a pretty fine main chick who doesn't have much to do but looks nice not doing it. I'd sure like to stick something in her little Dutch oven. All told, probably the best Xmas movie since *Bad Santa*.

Santa and the Three Bears
(1970)

I guess the forest ranger in this Christmas special doesn't have any family or friends, because he spends all his time wandering around talking to himself or occasionally to the local bears. He's not a very good park ranger, either, since he goes out and illegally cuts down a Christmas tree for his own use. What, you think the law doesn't apply to you because you wear a uniform? Typical. Anyway, when the ranger tells these bear cubs about Christmas they start spazzing out and their mom can't hibernate, so finally she goes to "have a talk with that Mr. Ranger". I figured she was gonna maul the shit out of him, which would've been awesome (and frankly she'd probably be doing the poor, lonely bastard a favor - he actually wrapped Christmas gifts for *himself* and put them under the tree). That's not what happens though. Instead, the ranger agrees to dress as Santa and visit the bears so they can have Christmas too. He takes a nap first, though, and when he wakes up *these faces in the fire are singing to him*. **What the fuck???** You know what? I don't think those bears can talk at all - I think this guy has just completely flipped his lid. Irregardless, he's a man of his word and he attempts to deliver some Christmas gifts to the bears even though there's a fucking blizzard going on. I'm sure in his untethered mind he's doing a kindness, so it's too bad he'll probably end up dying alone and no one will find the body until long after his bear "friends" eat most of it and he can't be identified. Jesus Christ, what a depressing cartoon.

Santa Baby

(2006)

Santa suffers a heart attack, so his daughter Jenny McCarthy has to save Christmas. For a standard-issue Xmas movie this one is pretty tolerable: there's actually a couple of funny parts, two people who aren't even important to the story get it on in Santa's workshop for absolutely no reason (of course we don't see them naked or anything, but just knowing somebody did the nasty on some kid's toys is good enough for me), and nobody says anything particularly puke-inducing. Also I liked Lucy the elf - she was pretty damn cute. The elves in this flick are all identified as retarded (seriously), but I'm not above fucking a retarded elf, as long as she's hot. Same goes for midgets.

Santa Claus
(1985)

These elves rescue a jackass who's trying to deliver toys during a blizzard, take him to the North Pole, and teach him to be Santa Claus. The first half of this movie is fucking awful: the main elf is Arthur 2 on the Rocks (one of the biggest douchebags of all time); the "jokes" are shit like "He just needs a little **elf** control." (I hope whoever wrote that is getting raped in prison right now. Seriously.); and when they want us to feel sorry for this homeless kid they show him with his face pressed against the window of a McDonald's (I'm surprised they didn't have him sing a song about how much he loves Chicken McNuggets during this part). The best though is when the homeless kid actually meets Santa - instead of helping him out in any practical way, Santa just takes him for a quick ride in his sleigh and then sends him packing! Maybe he was all out of Christmas miracles, but you'd think he could at least slip the kid five bucks for a sandwich or something. Oh well, he probably would've just spent it on booze anyway.

The second half is even worse. Arthur 2 on the Rocks runs away, teams up with a toymaker who's so evil he designs stuffed animals that have nails and broken glass in them (duh), and helps him invent lollipops that grant the power of flight to whoever eats them. Goddammit, that's so fucking piss-stupid it's a fucking *insult*. And it gets even dumber! There's a flying car, exploding candy canes, a guy who floats off into outer space but doesn't die, and Santa making a huge production out of doing a loop-de-loop with his sleigh to save some people who are falling when he could've achieved the exact same thing without all the fancy showboating and bullshit. *How stupid does this movie think we are???* Fuck you *Santa Claus*, you ass-reaming piece of *shit*. *Fuck you fuck you fuck you fuck you and rot in piss hell while you're sucking my (huge) fucking cock. I HATE THIS CUNT MOVIE.* Supposedly it cost like 50 billion dollars to make, so it's fucking awesome that when it first came out it totally tanked and everybody involved took the bath of a lifetime. Ah ha ha ha ha ha ha! Justice is served, you goddamned hacks. It truly was a Christmas miracle.

Santa Claus is Back in Town

(2008)

Holy crap, they have Christmas in France? I thought they just celebrated fucking "Bastille Day" and Frog Awareness Month. The shit you learn, right? So anyway, this flick begins with two Santa Clauses robbing several houses on Christmas Eve. The best part is when this little girl catches them and they try to pretend they really are Santa and his assistant: they've done this bit in movies a million times before, but this time the girl is an obnoxious brat who flips out when they don't have the present she asked for so the situation spirals completely out of control and it's fucking hilarious. Later they repent and decide to give some of the stuff they ripped off to the poor, but of course no good deed goes unsodomized so by the time it's all over they've been held hostage, robbed, and somebody's head gets blown off with a shotgun. Best of all, *nobody saves Christmas*, which means you can show this movie to your kids and tell them that this means that Christmas is officially canceled. Think of all the money you'll save.

Santa Clause Conquers the Martians
(1964)

That's what it says on the screen, Santa *Clause*. Jesus fucking Christ. So, this is one of those flicks everyone has heard of, but most people have the good sense to not actually watch. It all starts when the Martians decide that in addition to women Mars needs Santa Claus(e). They fly to Earth, bust into his workshop, and kidnap his fat ass, then put him to work in a Martian toy factory pushing buttons (why one of the Martians couldn't have been assigned to push the buttons, thus eliminating the need for all this skulduggery, is never explained). Santa must have an advanced case of Stockholm Syndrome because he has no problem whatsoever with any of this, but eventually everyone just gets bored with the whole idea and they let him go home. The end. It's a boring, stupid movie, but I did like the irritable Martian with the perpetual bad attitude. This is probably his best line:

REGULAR MARTIAN: "You can't dismiss the wisdom of centuries!"
IRRITABLE MARTIAN: "I can."

Also there's a Pia Zadora upskirt shot, but she's only ten here so forget you just read that.

The Santa Clause 2

(2002)

Even I must reluctantly admit that *The Santa Clause* was a pretty good idea for a movie. I mean, the guy from *Home Improvement* murders Santa and then has to take his place? That's fucking awesome. But Part 2? Is that really necessary? After seeing this piece of crap I can assure you that it is NOT. This time Home Improvement Santa has two problems (three, if you count how much this movie sucks): first he has to deal with his kid, who's on the "naughty" list for vandalizing the school to impress some girl (she's pretty goddamned cute though, so I fully support him in this); second, he has to get married by Christmas or everything's fucked (why nobody informed him of this before Thanksgiving is a mystery; maybe it's because this movie is stupid). Meanwhile the toys still need to get made – which is primarily achieved via child labor, but apparently Santa needs to be there in person to inspire them or dole out beatings or something – so they create a duplicate Santa. But, because this movie isn't complicated enough already, the duplicate goes mad with power and instigates a military coup! Ha! Unfortunately they never take this to its logical extreme (elf concentration camps) and that whole subplot just ends up being an excuse for some stupid *Speed 3* type action movie crap during the climax, which is this movie's substitute for actually having a climax. (I don't know what your girlfriend's excuse for not having a climax is. Maybe you should ask her.) It's all a just pointless waste of time - they should've called it "Santa Clause 2: The Lost Clause". Or better yet they should've skipped making it altogether and sent me the money, which I would've put to much better use by purchasing some really old scotch and some really young hookers.

The Santa Clause 3 The Escape Clause
(2006)

What the fuck is the deal with these *The Santa Clause* sequels? Each one has enough plot for six movies, enough story for none, sucks and is totally annoying, and yet somehow they're popular enough that the guy from *Home Improvement* has managed to coast on them for like a decade. Between the main plot, the subplot, and the mini-sub plot, there's so much pointless shit going on that you barely notice the one or two things that are almost clever (Santa's ringtone, Jack Frost's icicle tie). It still finds a way to be boring as hell though, and way too much of it is just an excuse to show off Santa's pad/workshop *MTV Cribs* style. Sorry, but I don't give a damn how many vending machines are in the elf break room. And does this movie really need three climaxes? I especially hated the one where the little girl saves her parents by melting Jack Frost's heart with love. My flood insurance isn't even gonna begin to cover all the damage caused by the puke that was responsible for.

I totally sympathize with the title though. If I was one of the actors contractually obligated to be in the next 15 of these shitfests, I'd sure be looking for an escape clause.

Santa Claws
(1996)

This is another one where a kid sees his mom getting porked by Santa Claus, so he goes insane, dresses up as Santa himself, and kills a bunch of people. I don't know about you, but I am *over* killer Santas trotting out this same, tired excuse. Really, what the fuck is so traumatic about seeing mom get a little XXXmas action? Wouldn't it be a lot worse if you caught your *dad* fucking Santa Claus? Or better yet, how about a movie where someone goes crazy because when he was a kid *he* got it from Santa, right up the ass? ("*Sob* I asked for a bike!") I'll tell you one thing, if just seeing your mom get a little action was enough to make you dress up as the guy and go on a killing spree, I would have dressed up as my dad's best friend and hacked my way through a gaggle of teenage chicks years ago. They need to give this tired-ass trope a fucking rest and come up with a new shtick.

This killer Santa is concentrating his rampage on some porno producers, so at least there's a lot of naked chicks, and they're all pretty hot (especially the first one who gets iced). The murder scenes are all pretty weak though, so this one really isn't worth your while unless your only two requirements for a movie are that it 1) be about Christmas and 2) have a lot of tits in it.

Santa Steps Out
(1998)
A novel by Robert Devereaux

I always like to slip at least one book review into these collections, because reading is fundamental, by which I mean fundamental to my bank account. In fact, right now might be a good time to take a break and buy the rest of my books, available wherever poorly-vetted books are sold. I promise you won't regret it. And even if you do, I don't care. No refunds.

So, Santa Claus bumps into the Tooth Fairy one evening and proceeds to fill her cavities with a little Christmas cheer. Sounds like some harmless fun, but the problem is – not unlike the kids in the cartoon *Angel's Friends* – this specific hookup was expressly forbidden by God. Why does God care who's boning who? (Seriously, Republicans, I'm asking you a legitimate question here.) Well, it turns out that scoring some fairy ass makes Santa Claus go old school, as in the Old Gods, and before long that other reappropriated Old God, the Easter Bunny, gets involved, and pretty soon all hell breaks loose. This sounds like a sacrilegious blast, and it is for a while, but by the time Mrs. Claus gets back at Santa by gang-banging every elf in his workshop it's all gotten so Johnny-try-too-hard that it's just ridiculous and, I hate to say it, kind of boring. Even if you're the type of person who enjoys childhood icon porn you'll probably be skimming by the halfway point. So for those of you who start this but can't be bothered to finish it, things ultimately work out just fine for Santa, but the Tooth Fairy comes to a horrifically bad end. Once again, the patriarchy punishes the mistress for a married man's indiscretions, while he gets off (heh) scot-free. Poor Tooth Fairy. She sounded like a pretty good time.

Santa Who?
(2000)

Santa falls out of his sleigh (the fucking drunk) and ends up with amnesia. Again? Now I haven't (legally) attended med school, but I would think that you might want to take someone in his condition to the hospital. Not the raging idiots in this movie though. Instead, they get him a job - as Santa! Ho ho ho! It's ironic! Christ. Anyway, some weird-looking elves eventually come looking for him, and the only funny part in the whole movie is when Customs gives them a bunch of shit. (And this was *before* 9/11. These days I doubt a guy who looks like the Vulcan from *Star Trek: Voyager*, two dorks, and a really creepy girl [?] elf who looks like her mom smoked crack throughout her pregnancy would be allowed into the country at all.) At least there's some decent eye candy: the main chick is pretty fine (I'd sure like to drive her eight tiny reindeer), and Santa's two little helpers at the mall are smokin'. Too bad we never see any of them naked.

Santa's Last Christmas
(1999)

This sounds tantalizingly ominous but don't get your hopes up. The story begins on Xmas Day, with Santa wrapping up his deliveries and setting the alarm clock for the crack of autumn, because apparently Santa and his elves *sleep* through the rest of the year. Seriously? I'd think an operation like his would have to be up and running 24/7, 365. He *must* be farming the piecework out to the Chinese. Anyway, come December 1st a local anthropomorphic mail bear (no, I spelled that right) notices that Santa hasn't been collecting his letters. He decides to investigate and discovers that there was some trouble with a space heater and Santa and the elves are all dead of carbon monoxide poisoning. Ha ha! Of course I'm bullshitting you, but that would've been a great twist, am I right? Actually the alarm didn't go off and they all overslept, which means that there's only time to make toys for *some* of the world's children. Tough break, non-white kids. Looks like they need a Christmas miracle, and they get one in the form of "Perk-Up Powder", which, once it kicks in, gets the elves so fucking high that they imagine little wooden homunculi are helping them make the toys in record time, when they obviously did it all themselves in an hours-long burst of drug-fueled mania. Result: Christmas is saved. Moral: Drugs are awesome.

Santa's Slay

(2005)

When they first started making killer Santa Claus movies in the 1980s people got pretty upset about it, and not a few frigid old ladies and pussy-whipped husbands protested and wrote angry letters to the editor and just generally disapproved in a self-important manner. These days they churn out a killer Santa Claus movie every other week and nobody even notices. This one features pro wrestler Goldberg as the killer Santa, and it's one of the better ones. The best parts are when he kicks a yippy little dog into a ceiling fan and when he kills the talentless fuck from *Saturday Night Live* who used to do that monkey boy sketch solely as an excuse to hump the hot guest star's leg. I hate that fucking pervert. Goldberg also kills the Nanny, which is sort of a mixed blessing because while she is annoying she hadn't gotten naked yet and you really need to see a chick who looks that good naked before she gets killed. So yeah, as killer Santa movies go, this one's a better-than-average B-. Of course, I consider *Silent Night, Deadly Night* **Part 2** to be an A+, so you might want to take that with a grain of salt.

The Search for Santa Claus
(1980)

I didn't know much about Santa Claus before I watched this documentary, but I always assumed he was invented by the Coca-Cola Company or possibly Al Gore. In this video though some old guy reveals the true story to a couple of little kids, which would be cute (I guess) except apparently the true story involves Santa Claus kicking the bucket, after which some jokers make off with his bones because the goddamn dune coons are coming and they're afraid they'll steal them (for what fucking reason I can't imagine, but whatever). He also discusses Santa's evil sidekick (source of all those tiresome Krampus movies, every one of which seems to think they're the first ones to come up with the idea), acknowledges the Old Gods (you know, like Yog-Sothoth), and informs the kids that Santa is the "patron saint" (that's a Catholic thing) of *thieves*. Jesus Christ, I'll bet those brats had nightmares for weeks. Obviously this tape is fucking awesome. On the back it says "This holiday classic will quickly join the ranks of Rudolph and Frosty as a Christmas tradition to be enjoyed in your home year after year," and if you have kids I think that's a pretty good idea. That'll learn the little bastards.

Secret Santa

(2003)

Due to convoluted circumstances and bad writing, Kelly from *Beverly Hills 90125* ends up spending her Christmas trying to unmask this hick burg's secret Santa. She eventually figures out who he is, but by then she's learned a valuable Christmas miracle so she decides not to reveal his identity. This movie's so by-the-numbers there's really nothing to do but sit back and watch the hackneyed events unfold. It's sad, because just by rearranging the letters in "Secret Santa" I can come up with a hundred movie ideas that sound way more interesting than this lame-ass, generic flick, from the super obvious ("Secret Satan") to the completely fucked up ("Acne Tasters"). Or how about this: Kelly from *Beverly Hills 90125* stars in... *Victoria's Secret Santa*. At least with a title like that there's a reasonable chance she'd show us her jingle bells.

Silent Night, Bloody Night
(1972)

This flick has gore, murders, revenge, and incest – all the shit people like – but somehow it manages to suck anyway. Maybe it's because it takes forever for anything cool to go down, and nothing happens in the meantime except people walking around and making phone calls. There is one impressively bloody axe murder early on, but other than that it's all pretty boring. Whoever was in charge of hot brunettes did a terrific job though: the main chick, the realtor's girlfriend, and even a completely inconsequential chick who's only onscreen for two seconds subbing at an old-school phone company's switchboard are all brunettes, and they are all beyond incredible. Too bad we never see any of them naked.

Silent Night Deadly Night
(1984)

Seeing your parents murdered by Santa Claus is bad enough, but being raised by Catholics *and* working retail during Christmas? No wonder this guy goes bonkers. The problem with this flick is that it takes way too long for our main guy to completely lose it - until then all we get is a violent robbery, a car-jacking, some tits, a throat slitting, some more tits, a little kid punching out Santa, the Krull board game (who knew?), Santa scaring a little girl who sits on his lap, even more tits, and some sexual assault. You know, I totally forgot what my complaint was. Anyway, when he finally does flip out it's nothing short of awesome: he strangles a guy with Xmas lights, stabs a topless hottie in the stomach, trepans his boss with a roofing hammer, shoots this broad with an arrow, impales another topless chick on some antlers, throws a dude through a window, decapitates a sledder, and axes a cop (not like when a black person "axes" you for directions, I mean with an actual axe). The end is even more brilliant: first the pigs blow away a completely innocent Santa in front of all these orphans, then they blow away the correct Santa...in front of the very same orphans! Can you imagine how fucked up those kids are gonna be? That's like twenty built-in sequels right there, although in reality they only managed five, I think, before they ran out of steam, of which Part 2 is considered the worst but is actually the best and you better believe I will die on this hill. *"Garbage day!"*

Homework Assignment: "Santa's Watching", the main song from this flick, sounds enough like a real, normal Christmas tune that you could totally trick your caroling party, or possibly even a church congregation, into adding it to their *repertoire*. Free ebooks to anyone who pulls this off and sends me video of it.

Silent Night Deadly Night 5 The Toy Maker

(1991)

A little boy watches as his dad is killed by a crazy, mechanical Santa Claus toy, so needless to say he develops some issues. When even Rambo cartoons can't snap him out of it, his mom tries to cheer him up by taking him to a toy store run by a guy named Pedo.

To reiterate: She takes her *young child*...to visit an adult...named *Pedo*.

She is in mourning, so I suppose we can excuse this particular lapse in judgment. But still. Anyway, there's some rigmarole and skulduggery in a pathetic attempt to red herring us, but the gist of it is that Pedo's son is building killer toys, which are fucking people up in gory but utterly ridiculous ways. Why is he doing this? Because in reality he's he's a full-on Westworld robot with interchangeable heads! (I realize that doesn't actually answer the question. If there was a stated reason, for any of this, I forget what it was.) Not weird enough? Okay, in the end the robot strips down and tries to rape the mom with his non-existent, Ken doll non-junk while screaming "I love you mommy!" *Jesus H. Christ* that's fucked up.

Can you imagine if Freud watched this movie? Nigga would explode. There's no tits – which is too bad because hotness abounds – but between that delirious non-rape and the part where Tony Award winner Mickey Rooney calls someone a son of a bitch before busting a whiskey bottle over their head, I think this qualifies as required viewing.

Single Santa Seeks Mrs. Claus
(2004)

Santa Claus Jr. (it's fucking Mahoney from *Police Academy*) has to get hitched, but he wants to find "someone who feels like the other half of my heart" (Jesus, that's it, I'm gonna hurl). I'm not exactly sure, but I think he just goes door to door asking broads to marry him until he accidentally meets Crystal Bernard. Crystal Bernard's impressed with his acting skills (I'll bet that's the first time *that* ever happened), so he helps her out with this commercial she's putting together and then he uses his Jedi Santa powers to create some bargain-basement Christmas miracles until he finally impresses his way into her pants. The best thing about this movie, by far, is Crystal Bernard's legs. By 2004 she was starting to hag out a *little* bit, but I still wouldn't balk at having those delicious stems wrapped around my waist. Other than that this flick is pretty worthless, and squanders any and all opportunities. I mean, Crystal Bernard ultimately becomes Mrs. Santa Claus and we don't even see her in a sexy Santa outfit! And does that mean she's gonna get fat now? That *really* fucking sucks.

A Snow White Christmas

(1980)

"Let's give this cartoon a little twist. Instead of the main chick being Snow White, we'll make her Snow White's *daughter*."

"Also named 'Snow White'?"

"Of course. No need to confuse everybody."

"I like that. We'll make her a teenager, really connect with the kids."

"Exactly."

"So if they have the same name, how do we differentiate her from her mom?"

"Well, mom ran around with seven dwarfs..."

"Right."

"So maybe her daughter hangs out with seven... midgets?"

"Ralph, that's the same thing."

"No, it isn't. A dwarf's body is disproportionate, whereas a midget's body is smaller than a normal person's, but proportionate."

"It's still too similar. Besides, I think they like to be called 'little people' now."

"'Little people'? Who'd want to be called that?"

"Well that's what I heard."

"What about elves? She could be friends with seven elves."

"Naw. Too fruity."

"Hmmm."

"Hmmm."

"Wait! I've got it! Seven *giants!*"

"Hey, yeah! Giants are the complete opposite of dwarfs!"

"And you know how teenagers are, always doing the exact opposite of their parents."

"Yeah, right? That's fucking brilliant. Wanna take an early lunch?"

"Hell, yes. We've earned it."

Snowglobe
(2007)

This hottie can't stand her family, and it's understandable because they're a bunch of obnoxious goombah fucks. If they were my family, I would move as far away from them as possible. And then call in an air strike. So one day a delivery guy drops off this mysterious snow globe that plays the theme from *Newhart*, and it turns out that the tiny little people inside of it are alive and she can teleport into the globe and hang out with them. It's like the Bottle City of Kandor, except instead of having superpowers everyone in the Bottle Town of Snowglobe is a naive, white bread, borderline retard who just *loves* Christmas. Man, I would give anything to visit this place - I could crush all resistance and take over in like an afternoon, and then all their tight-sweater-wearing women would be mine. Anyway, I was pretty sure I knew where this one was going (she learns a valuable lesson, Christmas is saved, everyone hugs, I puke on the floor, the dog licks a bunch of it up before I can get the mop, I beat the shit out of him), but then there's this huge twist that I *totally* didn't see coming. You know, I can't remember the last time that happened, and I'm not unimpressed. The problem though is that this movie can't be bothered to satisfactorily explore the ramifications of its weird premise. For example, what would happen to the

Bottle Town people if you put the snow globe in the microwave? It's a pretty safe bet that this is the sort of thing someone watching this movie would like to know, but it isn't even addressed. If I wanted to sit through a movie that sets up a bunch of cool shit then defiantly refuses to follow through, I'd rewatch *The Matrix*.

Snowmageddon

(2011)

I've always wanted to see a movie where Christmas magic backfires, and I guess that's what's happening here. See, there's this magical snow globe that affects the real world, I guess so you can make it snow for real just in time for the holidays,* but for some reason it also causes random, non-existent natural disasters to occur, like firequakes and exploding ice storms. The result: precarious, disaster movie predicaments, like being trapped in a helicopter that's about to slide over a cliff, or trapped in a bus that's been electrified by downed power lines, or trapped watching this idiot parade of nonsense. The default main guy finally decides that the snow globe has to go (well done, Holmes), so, like a common Hobbit, he trudges up the side of the local volcano and drops it in. Why a volcano? Because that's how it works in the board game his kid plays. Yeah, I don't see the connection either. This entire flick exists in some surreal tard world that only the person who wrote it understands, and to try to make sense of it (or why anyone would actually cough up the bread to make it) can only lead to madness. Just more proof that there will never be a decent movie that ends in "-mageddon".

*Those of us who drive drunk during the holidays don't appreciate this, by the way.

Starlight Night
(1939)

Wow, approved by the Legion of Decency. This should be sexy. It starts by informing us that this is the "historic and authentic account" of the song "Silent Night, Holy Night", but then immediately derails into a bunch of rigmarole about this old goat who's p.o.'ed because his daughter wants to start a family with some joker who once fought for Napoleon, and if there's one thing he hates, it's that son-of-a-bitch Napoleon. He just never got over the siege of Toulon. She goes through with it anyway and the old man disowns the lot of them, but suddenly, years later, there's an avalanche! I hope you're following this, because I'm not. The estranged family loses everything in the avalanche and goes to the old man for help, but he tells them to fuck off so they end up sleeping in a barn. Fortunately for them though the local padre lays a major, and very public, guilt trip on the old man at Christmas mass, so he caves and, presumably, writes them a check or something.

And that's the historic and authentic story of "Silent Night, Holy Night". Apparently.

The Tits That Saved XXX-mas
(2003)

Good hustle, but the unfortunate truth is that there are entirely too many fakes in this movie. My great-grandmother always used to say that Christmas just stopped feeling like Christmas when people switched from real, natural Christmas trees to artificial ones. I feel the same way about tits.

To All a Goodnight

(1980)

This movie takes place at a finishing school for girls, but I guess they're not quite finished yet because they're all still ugly as fuck. Ha ha! Anyway, this guy is phenomenally pissed off that some hottie died in a flashback, so he dresses up as Santa Claus and starts murdering everybody. And I can't say I blame him, because she really was the only hottie in this entire movie. Since there's no reason to see the rest of the cast naked this one really needs to deliver in the gore department, but they *schtupped* that pony too because the murders are weaker than a *Rick and Morty* fan's game. Why even make a slasher movie if you don't plan on going all out on the murders? Obviously the people behind this didn't have anywhere near enough Christmas spirit.

And seriously, they couldn't find *any* other hot chicks to be in this?

Together Again for the First Time
(2008)

A family gets together for Christmas, and they all fight. This is always entertaining, and even though it doesn't approach the levels I grew up with (Xmas tree dragged upstairs and thrown out a second story window; someone dry-clicking a revolver in a teenage girl's face) I laughed out loud at least twice, which is more than I can say for most holiday movies. And Christ but you won't believe the hotness on hand: the main guy's British girlfriend and the dumb sister with the fiancé are just run-of-the-mill hot, but I'd hang my Christmas balls all over the bitchy redhead, and the relatively normal brunette sister is so incomprehensibly tasty that I'd [CENSORED]. (My new editor nixed that one so let's just say that it involves two giant novelty candy canes, a bucket of chum, and all of her orifices. ALL of them.) Hell, the mom is the maid from *Newhart* (you remember, the one who looked like a non-slutty Samantha Fox), and even she's still shockingly doable. There was some crying and drama and *Oh-my-god-you're-on-drugs!* towards the end, but as far as I'm concerned that just made it even more Christmasy. I give it two candy canes up. *Right up that hot brunette's eager little [CENSORED] and then [CENSORED] with both of my [CENSORED] [CENSORED] and [CENSORED] on fucking fire, that is.*

Okay, this new editor isn't working out at all. If you're reading this, Kevin, you can pick up your last check on Monday. Don't cash it for a couple of days though, okay?

A Town Without Christmas
(2001)

A mystery kid writes a letter to Santa Claus threatening to kill himself if his dad doesn't get a job for Christmas, so and endless stream of reporters and gawkers invade the hick-ass burg the letter was postmarked from, trying to figure out who the kid is. Okay, first of all, I notice that this letter got delivered without any postage, which is bullshit. I pay my taxes. Second, I pulled this same stunt when I was little in a bid for some additional Xmas loot and it sure as hell didn't turn into a goddamn media circus. Instead, when my dad found out, he gave me one of my presents early: an ass beating. If you ask me, this kid is getting all the breaks. Anyway, it turns out *everyone* in this town is on hard times. Some of them are so broke, in fact, that they're reduced to auctioning off their personal belongings in the street.

Yes, I laughed out loud at this point.

But I wasn't laughing for long, because after this old lady sells her beloved music box for a hundred and fifty big ones and then stands there looking all brokenhearted until someone buys it back for her I finally figured it out: *there is no kid*. These yokels are just running a classic burn on everybody! I'll bet that ol' lady sells her "treasured" music box four or five times a week. You know who probably wrote that "suicidal kid" letter? The fucking mayor. And sure enough, when a kid finally steps forward to take the credit/blame it's *the mayor's daughter*. The movie tries to pretend that it's all a Christmas miracle, but they're not fooling Mr. Satanism - this was an intricately-planned grift from day one. Pay attention to the old dude who subtly steals the main guy's credit card towards the end: these are fucking professionals. What a bunch of scumbags. They should've called it "A Town Without Scruples".

The Toy that Saved Christmas
(1996)

Veggie Tales is insidious, because at first you might not even realize it's trying to trick you into simping for Jesus. If you never heard of *Veggie Tales*, let me explain. See, Christians have this whole insane parallel entertainment universe featuring their own music, TV shows, movies, books, and who knows what the fuck else, all of which is somewhat similar to regular versions of that stuff, except Christian. It's kind of like how Canada has its own Top 40 similar to yet entirely separate from America's Top 40, and when you visit Canada there's all these bands on the radio you never heard of before, and groups like Men Without Hats still have shit on the charts. Anyway, *Veggie Tales* is a kids' show about living vegetables with big googly eyes (Mr. Potato Head lawsuit pending) who love Jesus. In this episode, the latest must-have Christmas toy is possessed by the ~~Devil~~ Holy Spirit, comes to life, and helps everyone learn the true meaning of Christmas, which is pretty much the same as the true meaning of Christmas in any other cartoon, except they name-drop Jesus more. There's also an evil cucumber (Wait, the bad guy's a vegetable too? Shouldn't he be, I dunno, a vegetarian or something?), and a part where they mock the IRS.

(It's bad enough church doesn't pay taxes, but do they have to rub our faces in it?) Frankly it's all pretty surreal and I'm not sure I even understand it. I mean, are these vegetables talking about the same Jesus my girlfriend is always screaming for when we fuck, or do they have their own vegetable messiah who was presumably diced up and grilled for their sins? Or maybe the Veggie Tales Jesus is what regular Jesus was eating during that Last Supper deal. Man, that's fucked up. And I thought Gnosticism was difficult to understand.

The Trolls and the Christmas Express
(1980)

Trolls, disguised as elves,* infiltrate Santa's village on a mission of sabotage. Their first target is the toy assembly line, but Santa's quality control is too efficient so the trolls switch to Plan B - they keep the reindeer up all night partying so on Christmas Eve they pass out mid-flight and Santa's sleigh crashes. It looks like the trolls have won, but then Santa just delivers his presents via train, even though that presumably entails building thousands of miles of train track across the *open ocean*. Logic be damned, you just can't beat Santa Claus. The trolls manage to make more trouble, but then they blow their cover at which point Santa and his elves use spurious logic and homonyms to get them to switch sides. It's probably the first time Christmas has ever been saved by a homonym, and hopefully the last; next time something like this goes down I expect Santa break out the heavy artillery.

*I know this isn't very woke of me, but I've never been able to tell the difference.

12 Dates of Christmas
(2011)

Made-for-TV Christmas movies never get tired of ripping off *Groundhog Day*. It's like they're trapped in their own Groundhog Day of creativity. This time our main chick is reliving the same blind date, on Xmas Eve, over and over again. Unapologetically derivative crap, sure, but the main chick is Amy Smart (still rocking my favorite Smart ass), and the main guy is none other than Zack Morris, who fully redeemed himself with the brilliant, underrated *Dead Man on Campus* and now sits amongst the cool elite as far as I'm concerned. So, good cast...good (stolen) premise... *great* legs (I love you, Amy). Clearly there are worse Christmas movies I could be subjecting myself to. Like anything that involves cute animals saving it.

Oh, and bonus points for the dead wife who died falling off a roof, instead of being yet another uninspired drunk-driving casualty. What does it say about movie industry people when they all seem to think that the only way anyone ever dies is via drunk driving?

Unaccompanied Minors
(2006)

This one got on my good side immediately by using the Kinks' "Father Christmas" as the theme song and trotting out, as one of the main minors, a particularly fine example of underage hotness. Rest assured, my interest in her is purely statutory. The story's so random that eventually it ceases to exist, and it's not particularly funny, but the bad guys are airport security so at least it's realistic, and there's tons of famous people on hand, like (Everybody Hates) Chris, Fez from *That '70s Television Program*, the fat Indian girl from *The Office*, and that one comedian who yells all the time. (No, not that comedian who yells all the time. The other one.) Plus they worked in this whole, inexplicable "saving the environment is stupid" message, which I found particularly hilarious. So, okay, I guess it is a little funny.

Up on the Housetop
(1992)

Holy shit, this Christmas cartoon special is actually, occasionally funny. Our main guy is tired of Christmas and all the bullshit it entails, and when he finds out that his family won't be flying in for Xmas dinner (dad's stuck in Florida on a deathwatch, his brother is in Minneapolis partying with some coked-up rock whores) he gets even more depressed until Santa Claus shows up and teaches him the true meaning of blah blah blah. It's the same old story, but along the way it bashes local news and their wretched Christmas fluff pieces, the goddamned Salvation Army, *It's a Wonderful Life* being on every fucking channel (thank god those days are over), and even Christmas cartoon specials ("Frankenstein Saves Christmas"). Plus they work in a really gross psoriasis joke. I don't want to give the impression that this isn't, in it's own way, cheap crap (most of the action consists of the main guy walking from left to right across the screen), but at least it wasn't total puke bait from start to finish. As far as Christmas specials go, that puts it in something like the top 3%.

A Very Brady Christmas
(1988)

The grown-up Brady Bunch kids and their obnoxious Brady Bunch families all fly in to spend Christmas at the Brady Bunch house. Even Alice comes back (from the grave, it looks like), although she's obviously completely fucking senile: she dresses as a maid the entire time she's there, despite the fact that she doesn't even work for them anymore! As if that isn't enough to deal with, one of the kids has dropped out of school, another one's heading for divorce, another one's bum husband just got fired... Now in real life the second any of this came to light there would be a vicious argument with people screaming shit like "I *never* thought you were good enough for my daughter!" or "Don't you *dare* talk to your mother that way, you *fucking ingrate!*", but does that happen here? Of course not; instead, they solve every single problem during a nice little chat over dinner. Who ever heard of a family Christmas that didn't involve drinking, crying, guilt, threats, pettiness, and at least one fistfight? Leave it to the Bradys to spit on all these traditions. The worst is yet to come though: later a building collapses on Dad Brady, and after every other rescue attempt fails the Brady Bunch sing a Christmas song and suddenly he pops out of the rubble completely unharmed! You know, there's a point when a movie is just pissing in your fucking face and this one crossed it right there. Screw the Bradys - if it wasn't for Jan and (adult) Cindy's combined fine-itude I'd order a hit on the lot of them.

Yogi Bear's All-Star Comedy Christmas Caper
(1982)

Take it from me kids, nothing good ever comes of a caper. Yogi Bear's friends stop by Jellystone Park for a Christmas visit, his friends consisting of all those cartoon characters everybody recognizes but nobody can actually identify. You know, there's that gay lion who looks sort of like the Pink Panther, the father & son dog duo, the horse in the cowboy hat... Those jokers. Anyway, it turns out Yogi isn't even there - he escaped and is running around the "big city" engaging in antics (example: kidnapping). It's your typical half-assed Christmas Special garbage; the only really interesting thing that happens is that Fred Flintstone and Barney Rubble show up, because, amazingly enough, the gay lion actually calls them out since they're from prehistoric times and this should be impossible. In response, Fred and Barney rope the lion into a charity scam, and then beat the crap out of him.

You know, if this whole holiday was as bizarre as that one interaction in this dumb cartoon, I might actually enjoy it.

Bonus:

Here's some jokes/observations that got edited out of the reviews in this book. See if you can guess which entries they were cut from!

*That is, if my parents actually bought Christmas presents ("A day without a beating **is** a present." -My Dad).*

It's a Christmas sucktacular!

Learning there's a sequel to _____ is like finding out you've got the sack cancer.

Isn't it illegal to be that Jewish on Christmas?

...and Jokes so old that Edison wouldn't have used them.

Santa coming down his own chimney. Damn that sounds perverted.

Milton Keynes UK
Ingram Content Group UK Ltd.
UKHW021041031224
452078UK00010B/569